Liz M

P9-CFD-425

School Leader's Guide to

Root Cause Analysis

Using Data to Dissolve Problems

Paul G. Preuss, Ed.D.

EYE ON EDUCATION

6 DEPOT WAY WEST, SUITE 106

LARCHMONT, NY 10538

(914) 833–0551

(914) 833–0761 fax

www.eyeoneducation.com

Copyright © 2003 Eye On Education, Inc.

All Rights Reserved.

For information about permission to reproduce selections from this book, write: Eye On Education, Permissions Dept., Suite 106, 6 Depot Way West, Larchmont, NY 10538.

Library of Congress Cataloging-in-Publication Data

Preuss, Paul G., 1942-
    School leader's guide to root cause analysis : using data to dissolve problems / Paul G. Preuss.
        p. cm.
    Includes bibliographical references and index.
    ISBN 1-930556-53-5
    1. Educational evaluation--United States. 2. educational leadership--United States. 3. School management and organization--United states. 1. Title.

LB2822. 75.P74 2003
379.1'58--dc21
10 9 8 7 6 5 4   2002040796

About the Author

Dr. Paul G. Preuss has completed 36 years of service in the public schools of New York State as teacher, principal, superintendent, and as assistant Board of Cooperative Educational Services (BOCES) superintendent. He coauthored the Unified Planning Process, which served as a basis for New York's Comprehensive District Education Planning process (CDEP), and established and directed the New York State Technical Assistance Center for Comprehensive District Education Planning. He remains a member of the New York State CDEP Steering Committee and the Steering Committee of the New York State Data Analysts Group. In retirement, he provides consulting services to school districts and not-for-profit agencies, and presents his ideas both locally and nationally.

Dr. Preuss holds degrees from Muhlenberg College, Colgate University, and Syracuse University. He is a student of organizational behavior and has become a systems thinker. His work is backed by 32 years of administrative experience in making positive things happen for students.

Foreword

We need this book!

With the No Child Left Behind Act, and with more schools and school districts getting into data analysis work each year, we are hearing educators wanting to learn how to determine "root causes" and how to perform "root cause analyses." Until now, there was no education-related book dedicated to the topic.

I am pleased to introduce the premier education book on the topic of root cause analysis— *School Leader's Guide to Root Cause Analysis*. Dr. Paul Preuss has done a fabulous job of showing us many examples from many different perspectives. The examples will ring familiar and be helpful to school board members, district and school administrators, teachers, and students. The Guide is easy to use, practical, based on real schools, and makes sense out of complicated events.

Dr. Preuss states in this text, "Too often we do not discuss and reflect on our practices." With this guide, educators everywhere will learn how to reflect on proactive positive results, as well as the reactive negative results. The Guide summarizes the theory and process of root cause analysis, while sharing learnings from real examples. The Guide, through Dr. Preuss' expertise, shows us how to solve the deep-rooted problems that perplex our educational systems and that keep us from getting the results we want. With the help of The Guide, educators can learn how to solve the real challenges of ensuring every child's learning, as opposed to solving the most obvious symptoms and seeing the same results year after year.

Dr. Preuss draws on his vast educational experience at all levels of education, his insights from working with all educational levels, and the knowledge he gained from some of the world's greatest systems thinkers to deliver his powerful message.

School Leader's Guide to Root Cause Analysis is designed to assist all who seek to improve learning for students through identifying and dissolving causes for student learning failure. I invite you to enjoy this treasure, and join me in commending Dr. Paul Preuss for his tremendous contribution to education.

Victoria L. Bernhardt
Executive Director
Education for the Future
vbernhardt@csuchico.edu
http://eff.csuchico.edu

Acknowledgments

In my professional life, I have been very fortunate to be surrounded by people who are brighter and more experienced and knowledgeable than I. This has provided me with a very rich environment in which to learn and to grow. I am thankful and appreciative of their contributions to the continuing development of my own abilities, part of which I now hope to pass on through this guide to root cause analysis.

Over the last several years I have had the good fortune to work with many who I now consider as colleagues at the New York State Education Department such as Barbara Flynn, Pat Gabriel, Kathy Ordway, Helen Branigan, David Payton, Isabel Pickett, Mary Pillsworth and Assistant Commissioner James Butterworth. Before his retirement, Assistant Commissioner Sam Corsi provided me with necessary encouragement. He was a constant source of motivation through his personal commitment to making schools a better place for all students. Barbara Flynn continues to coordinate the Comprehensive District Educational Planning process (CDEP) pilot for the State Education Department, and I am grateful for her help in reviewing this manuscript.

At the Herkimer Board of Cooperative Educational Services (BOCES), I was supported and encouraged in my eight years as Assistant BOCES Superintendent for Instruction and Planning by both my superintendents, William Whitehill and John Stoothoff. I dare not forget Joyce Christiano, Director of the Mohawk Regional Teachers Center, and Walt Lallier, Director of our regional SETRC (Special Education Training and Resource Center) with whom I codeveloped the original "Unified Planning Process." Unified Planning metamorphosed into what became New York's Comprehensive District Educational Planning process (CDEP). The search for root cause is an essential element of both processes My years at BOCES were filled with many hours of direct contact with our 12 component superintendents, the many board of education members, principals, and teaching staff, who made my life richer and my thoughts more grounded in the reality of everyday school life. Joseph Fusco, retired superintendent of the Ilion Central Schools, was most helpful in reviewing the draft manuscript.

One of my more valued associations has been membership in New York's Staff and Curriculum Development Network (SCDN). What a group! The doers of New York State. I want to name them all but must single out Bruce O'Connell, Carol Jacunski, Jim Collins, Jim Frenck, Joan Daly-Lewis, Marilyn Gates-Kurzawa, John Gangemi, Pru Posner, Karla Reiss, Jane Bullowa, Robin Elliser, Ed Zero, and Diane DiMaria. Many others have been an inspiration to me through their dedication to the improvement of learning throughout our state.

The CDEP Steering Committee has been a constant source of support and guidance. Many of those listed above are members, but, in addition, Stu Horn, Larrilee Jemiola, Sharon Funk, Robert Harris, Elaine Zseller, Theresa Bucci, Brian Preston, Ted Smith, and Sean Brady have been stalwarts. I should not pass over the contributions of our consultant from England, Andy Smith.

The New York State Data Analysts Group has been a more recent source of wisdom and understanding, and I have been fortunate to serve on that group's steering committee as well. Those much more versed than I in the use of numbers have been tolerant of my generalist's questions and probing of the deeper mysteries of assessment and analysis of scores.

Then there are the many school districts with which I consult and their dedicated leaders and staff who are seeking ways to improve learning. I hope that I impart at least as much as I have learned from each experience.

Writers and national presenters such as James Leonard, William Glasser, Jack Oxenrider, and Russell Ackoff have made indelible impressions on my thinking. I have come to know Victoria Bernhardt as a fellow traveler on the road to school improvement. She is owed special gratitude both for her insights and her encouraging me to complete this task. Others, such as Peter Senge, W. Edwards Deming, Don Wheeler, and Edie Holcomb, I have come to know and appreciate only vicariously through their books. Nevertheless, each of these have contributed substantially to my thinking and practice.

In this day of the Internet, I have learned much from researching its contents related to causal analysis—most particularly from the Root Cause Conference and its many members, especially Bob Nelms, Bill Corcoran, Lawrence Leach, and Bob Latino.

Finally, I have been provided the necessary support, understanding, and encouragement to continue in this work during my "retirement" years by my wife Becky. She is tolerant of my absences when I have to travel, and, when home, of my many hours in my office writing or researching. Becky recently retired from a lifetime of teaching in elementary schools. Many times, perhaps unknowingly, she has also provided me with continuing unique insights into the daily life of classroom teachers. She also is a very fine proof reader who has helped me with the preparation of my final draft.

So, you see, I have received a very good measure of professional and home support. It is my hope that through this guide I can pass on the best of what I have learned for the benefit of your students.

Table of Contents

Introduction

Although the trend toward greater use of school data has been underway for several years, the recent federal "No Child Left Behind" legislation has made the use of school data a certainty for all. Now the most common issues are: which data to use and how to use them appropriately to arrive at sound decisions. All too often, data are the stimuli for "knee-jerk" reactions by those involved with school improvement efforts that jump from problem to solution without investigating cause. Without pausing for reflecting on cause, solutions are often aimed at the wrong issues and thereby waste precious time and resources while causing unintended consequences themselves. The purpose of this educator's guide to root cause analysis is to provide all school personnel with basic information, examples, and processes that can be used to seek root cause for problems. Once identified, causes can be dissolved or diminished using proper strategies aimed at that purpose, and school performances and outcomes for students can be more efficiently improved. Although the primary focus of this text is on issues related to student academic performance, root cause analysis can be used in all areas of school operations.

Perhaps as recently as 10 years ago, this text might have been called *A Principal's Guide to Root Cause Analysis*. This can no longer be the case. Today's effective school must rely upon leadership that is distributed widely and that is called upon regularly to resolve specific issues of school improvement. Successful school leadership can no longer be confined to a single position or level of hierarchy within the system. This guide is written for all who seek to improve learning for all students.

For the school board, root cause analysis should become a key tool not only in understanding how to arrive at decisions to improve student learning, but also a key tool for effective management of school policies, facilities and finances.

For instructional staff, root cause analysis should be used to identify issues related to individual students, groups of students, and class cohorts, as well as issues impacting the school as a whole. Site management teams and school improvement teams will benefit by having members who seek cause rather than assign blame or attempt to apply patches that allow underlying causes to continue.

For administrative staff, whether at the district or building level, root cause analysis is an excellent tool for focusing discussion and organizational effort on dissolving or removing barriers to student success.

For staff developers, the concepts and skills of root cause analysis need to be integrated into staff development programs at all levels. Root cause analysis training should become a priority as a foundation skill necessary for other attempts to improve student learning. Root cause analysis should be employed in the development of plans for staff improvement, and, in fact, staff improvement efforts are best when they are the outgrowth of school improvement planning that seeks to dissolve causes for failure.

For higher education, it would be beneficial to all concerned if teachers and administrators coming from college and graduate programs had the rudiments of root cause analysis firmly entrenched in their arsenal of skills and dispositions before assuming leadership roles in schools.

The information, concepts, and processes contained within this guide can be used successfully at all levels of the school system: classroom, department, program, building, or district. The value of the content is maximized, however, when the whole system (district) is engaged in a system-wide improvement process. The problem of high school dropouts, for example, may be exposed in the high school years, but the root causes for the problem are often found, and are best dissolved, in other parts of the system.

Although this guide focuses upon root cause, it contains supporting information related to the concept. I have become increasingly aware, for example, of the importance of identifying a school's "key indicators of student success" before embarking on any use of data or on a search for root cause in problem areas. Other concepts, such as the difference between "means and ends," are also covered. These two issues have been given their own section in Chapter 2. Other essential concepts, which provide either a context or foundation for better understanding of root cause, are explained in Chapter 5 in the section dealing with Foundations.

This guide serves as a starting point for those who are traveling the road toward improved learning for all students. It offers a basic understanding of the need for root cause analysis and the processes that can be used to seek cause within the educational context. It is hoped that eventually all educators will be able to internalize the concepts and skills associated with root cause analysis and integrate them into their daily work and decision making.

Paul G. Preuss, Ed.D.
November 2002

1

Root Cause Basics

Root cause analysis is an effective tool used both reactively, to investigate an adverse event that already has occurred, and proactively, to analyze and improve processes and systems before they break down.

> Root Cause in Health Care: Tools & Techniques,
> The Joint Commission on Accreditation of
> Healthcare Organizations

Why Root Cause Analysis?

♦ *Root Cause Analysis* (RCA) helps dissolve the problem, not just the symptom.

Often, schools approach the symptom, e.g., poor attendance, as if it were the problem rather than a result. By focusing on the symptom, strategies are often misdirected and the causes for the problem remain untreated—enabling the symptoms to remain or reemerge.

♦ Root cause analysis eliminates patching and wasted effort.

Symptoms are often "dealt with" by coming up with a patch to cover them or to deal with their consequences. Many so-called compensatory programs are simply patches on a system where the original effort to teach/learn has been unsuccessful. Patches add complexity to the system, require additional resources, and create additional work. All of this amounts to wasted effort.

♦ Root cause analysis conserves scarce resources.

By eliminating fundamental (root) causes, symptoms can be reduced or eliminated, thereby conserving the need for additional resources. Remedies that do not consider root cause often fail to eliminate the symptoms. Resources are usually thought of in terms of time, money, space and personnel. However, such resources as good faith effort, commitment, voluntary participation, and resolve must also be conserved.

♦ Root cause analysis induces discussion and reflection.

Too often, we do not discuss and reflect on our practices. Root cause analysis provides the means whereby discussion and reflection can take place in a nonthreatening and open context. The introspection, quality, and depth of root cause discussions exceed typical problem solving where conversations jump from symptom to solution. Opinions not founded on data are rejected until proven. Knee-jerk reactions to problems are greatly reduced, if not eliminated.

♦ Root cause analysis provides rationale for strategy selection.

We cannot fix something until we know what is wrong. By focusing on dissolving the most fundamental causes for problems, we can then select strategies that are properly targeted on the cause rather than on the symptom. By identifying the cause, one can justify strategies that are aimed at the cause rather than the symptom.

What is "Root Cause"?

Rather than assume knowledge of what a "root cause" is, let's first look at several definitions:

From the Savannah River Project (a nuclear power station):

Root Cause is "the most basic cause that can reasonably be identified, that we have control to fix, and for which effective recommendations for prevention can be implemented."

From Medical Risk Management Associates:

Root Causes are "the underlying causes of adverse outcomes."

From the Joint Commission on Accreditation of Healthcare Organizations:

Root Causes are "the basic or casual factors that underlie variation in performance, including the occurrence or possible occurrence of a sentinel (major) event."

From Business Solutions—The Positive Way:

Root Causes are the "basic cause or causes" of the problem or symptoms.

From "Total Quality Schools," by Joseph C. Fields:

A Root Cause is "the most basic reason the problem occurs."

Other organizations differentiate between "contributory" or "proximate" causes and root causes. Often, the most immediate or obvious cause is mistakenly identified as the root cause when, instead, it is simply the most proximate contributory cause, which itself has much deeper roots.

> **Example**: Often, blame is first centered on an individual. Although an individual may have indeed committed an error that resulted in a problem, a deeper cause may be found in areas such as: training of the individual, scheduling of the individual, assignment of duties, clarification of duties, supervision, work environment, or any one of a host of other issues. Most people involved in root cause analysis understand that the vast majority of root causes are system-based rather than individual-based.

For purposes of this guide, the following definition suffices:

> *Root Cause—the deepest underlying cause, or causes, of positive or negative symptoms within any process that, if dissolved, would result in elimination, or substantial reduction, of the symptom.*

Let's look at this definition again, this time highlighting and commenting on its various essential components:

> **Root Cause**—the *deepest* underlying *cause, or causes*, of *positive or negative symptoms* within any *process* that if *dissolved* would result in elimination, or substantial reduction, of the symptom.

> ♦ **Deepest**—this means that we really have to dig deep to find most roots. They usually are not the most immediate, obvious, or proximate causes. Often, they are three, four, or five layers down into the system.

> **Example**: A high school has a high number of local (general) diploma graduates. However, the state is requiring that 100 percent of graduates have academic diplomas within a few years. Taking a detailed look at the local diploma recipients, it is found that fully two-thirds either had exceeded academic diploma requirements or were close to them. Upon further investigation, it is found that guidance counselors, and even the high school principal, communicate to parents and students that the academic diploma is not necessary for college acceptance or future success. Emphasis is placed on SAT scores instead. In discussions with the counselors and principal, it is found that the system has never placed emphasis on academic diplomas, and, in fact, the school's personnel felt they were doing their duty in accordance with what they believed the school system and the community wanted. The district (system) had not communicated this change in goals to its staff.

A few people take issue with the use of the term "root cause" and prefer instead the concept of "causal analysis." Their reasoning is that the concept of "root cause" came out of an industrial mechanical environment that is not suited to education and that there are usually multiple causes rather than a single root. Obviously, I have chosen to stick with the concept of "root cause." I really do not care where it was first used because I believe the metaphor works in any context. I especially like the concept of "root" because it implies that we must dig deeply to find cause. To me, the term "causal analysis" facilitates the easy, knee-jerk response of "I know the cause—here it is," rather than demanding the *deep* search that is typically required.

♦ **Cause or causes**—School systems are social systems. They are far more complex than either mechanical or biological systems. For this reason, it is often impossible to isolate a single root cause, and often it is possible to identify several causes that in combination bring about a symptom. The good news is that often, by dissolving any one of the multiple root causes, the symptoms can be reduced or even eliminated.

Models and examples: I often think of the fire triangle. It takes three elements to make a fire: a source of combustion, oxygen, and a source of fuel. Take any one of the three away and a fire cannot start or continue to burn. Often, an air crash is the result of the convergence of separate events that in and of themselves would not have caused an accident but when placed in combination result in a disaster. It has been found, in some instances, that a student can "survive" any one deficient process within a school but that when faced with two, three, or more, the student quickly falls behind.

♦ **Positive or negative**—Our successes, as well as our failures, have root causes. By studying the roots for our successes, we may find strategies that can be applied to improving all of our processes.

Example: A school district successfully implements the IBM program "Writing to Read." In looking back at its experience, the district identifies the following strategies as contributory to the program's success: direct faculty involvement and agreement in adopting the program; "by the book" training, staffing, and assignment of resources in support of the program; benchmarking and adaptation of a model from another successful school; thorough parent information; and continuous administrative involvement and encouragement. Can these strategies be applied to future programs? You bet!

- **Symptoms**—In dealing with problems, symptoms are found at the surface. They are the "red flag" that draws attention to the issue. A symptom is usually a noticeable gap between expectations and reality.

  Example: A school district has a very high failure rate in ninth grade. Expectations are that most students will successfully transition from middle school to high school. The reality is that over 50 percent of all freshman fail at least one course during the year. The failure rate is the "red flag" as well as a symptom of deeper underlying causes. In order to eliminate the symptom, the deeper underlying root causes have to be dissolved.

- **Process**—All work is process. A simple process has a minimum of three elements: a) input, b) added value, and c) output.

  Example: Writing (and mailing) a letter is a process. It has certain elements of input, such as blank paper, a blank envelope, a pen, a stamp, a source for the address as well as concepts to be placed in the letter as content. Then there is the value added process of actually composing and writing the letter followed by the physical mailing of the previously isolated elements as a single product. The output is both the physically completed letter and the communication it contains. Once we can identify the input, value added, and the output, we can identify the process. Schools are composed of hundreds of processes—two of the large umbrella processes are teaching and learning.

- **Dissolve**—We have to concentrate on dissolving the root rather than "fixing" the symptom with a patch. Once the root is dissolved, the symptom will go away of its own accord. Patches just add complexity and cost to the system. Some people think that much of what we do in school is patching.

  Example: A school district was faced with a very high number of out-of-school suspensions. Its solution to the problem was to implement an in-school suspension program. This resulted in space, staff and energy being assigned to what essentially was a patch on the system. They never looked at causes for the suspensions in order to substantially reduce or eliminate them.

Perhaps this is more than you ever wanted to know about the definition of "root cause." Hopefully, however, it provides an adequate foundation upon which to move forward and will make some of what follows easier to understand. One more time:

Root Cause—the deepest underlying cause, or causes, of positive or negative symptoms within any process that, if dissolved, would result in elimination, or substantial reduction, of the symptom.

Modalities of Root Cause Analysis

The schematic in Figure 1.1 graphically portrays the four modalities of root cause analysis. Root cause analysis is very often conducted in the "negative reactive" modality. That is, it is seeking causes for existing problems. Rarely, if ever, do we think in terms of the "positive reactive" modality, i.e., what made this program a success? What really made it work? By using the "positive reactive" modality we can perhaps find roots that enabled success in one area that can be used to dissolve problems in another.

Figure 1.1. Modalities of Root Cause Analysis

	Reactive	*Proactive*
Negative	**Negative Reactive RCA** Seeks to identify and dissolve roots for existing problems Why did this happen? What is holding us back?	**Negative Proactive RCA** Seeks to identify and dissolve potential roots for future problems What fundamental root porcesses, beliefs, attitudes, skills, and knowledge, must we change to bring what we want to fruition?
Positive	**Positive Reactive RCA** Seeks to identify and replicate roots for existing success when appropriate Why was this program a success? What elements contributed to its success?	**Positive Proactive RCA** Seeks to identify and implant roots necessary for future success What fundamental root processes, beliefs, attitudes, skills, and knowledge, must we install to bring what we want to fruition?

To complete this paradigm we must consider both the "positive proactive" and "negative proactive" modalities.

The "positive proactive" modality, as seen in Figure 1.1, asks the question: "What roots will be necessary to achieve success in this new initiative?" It then seeks to plant these roots prior to the implementation of the initiative. This is sometimes difficult and might appear as putting the cart before the horse. In any event, such a process of forward thinking will strengthen any implementation, even if the roots are laid down as the implementation unfolds.

The "negative proactive" modality is the process of asking the negative, future-oriented question: "What roots will impede the implementation of this new initiative?" When properly thought out, the restraining roots can be dissolved prior to implementation.

For example, the central theme of Phillip Schlecty's action plan for educational reform can be summed up in terms of the "positive proactive" modality of root cause analysis. Schlecty states:

> "I have come to the conclusion that change is peculiarly difficult in schools because the schools, and the school districts of which they are typically a part, lack the capacities needed to support and sustain change efforts." (Schlecty, p. 80)

One can think of the absent "capacities" as root causes of future failure or, in the "positive proactive" modality, as "necessary for future success." Schlecty identifies these capacities and then goes into some depth explaining each one. They are:

- ♦ The capacity to establish and maintain a focus on the future.
- ♦ The capacity to maintain a constant direction.
- ♦ The capacity to act strategically.

When implementing root cause analysis itself, we should be thinking in the proactive mode and ask: What roots (capacities) will be necessary for success? What negative roots will cause failure?

As the beliefs, concepts and processes of root cause analysis become more internalized we will also begin to think and act in all four modalities. What follows are examples of each modality.

Examples of RCA Modalities

An Example of a "Positive Reactive" Modality

A school district successfully implemented IBM's writing-to-read program, whereas several neighboring districts had not succeeded. In reviewing the possible roots of the program's successful implementation, the following factors were identified:

- ♦ Staff were involved in the decision from the beginning.
- ♦ Staff were given the "power" to decide to implement the program.
- ♦ Staff were thoroughly trained to use the program.

- ◆ Administration gathered, and aligned, the necessary resources and saw to it that the program was implemented "by the book."

- ◆ Implementation was "benchmarked" with a successful school district and much was learned from that school district's experience.

- ◆ Parents were informed and involved as soon as possible.

- ◆ The program itself had been proven in many situations and was aligned with the district's own philosophy and beliefs.

The issue now becomes: What can we learn from this successful intervention that can be applied to future program implementations?

As an aside, and to be true to Chapter 2, the implementation of a program such as Writing to Read must be seen only as a means, not an end. A true evaluation of the program's success is not in its successful implementation but is in the program's impact on the key indicator it was implemented to address. In other words, are the students learning to read "better" now than they did before the program was implemented. Unfortunately it is far too typical that we stop at the measurement of implementation and do not continue to the evaluation of results.

An Example of a "Positive Proactive" Modality

When implementing RCA within a school building or district, the identification of supporting driving forces would be a first step. The question might be: "What do we have going for us that will enable the success of this process?" Depending upon the situation, answers might be such things as:

- ◆ Committed administrative leadership.

- ◆ Desire for improved student achievement on the part of staff.

- ◆ Needs to meet increased demands for accountability.

- ◆ Knowing what the key problem issues are.

- ◆ The technical infrastructure to properly analyze data.

A further question might be: "What can we apply to RCA that we learned from the successful implementation of Writing to Read?" Are there crossover elements?

An Example of "Negative Proactive" Modality

Building on the issue used above, we can, using the "Negative Proactive" modality, identify the restraining forces for the purpose of dissolving them. The question might then be: "What forces will hold us back from being successful in RCA?" Again, depending upon the situation, answers might be:

- The lack of extensive data.
- Severe time constraints.
- Lack of clerical support and analysis capabilities.
- The need for more training and, perhaps, facilitation of the team.

In order for the implementation of RCA to be successful, these restraining forces need to be dissolved or reduced to the point where they will not halt the implementation of RCA as a problem-solving process. Restraining forces are prioritized and an action plan is developed and agreed upon for each of the issues identified and agreed upon as a priority restraining force.

An Example of a "Negative Reactive" Modality

Most root cause analyses are conducted in this "problem-solving" mode.

A school district has a high failure rate in Math Level I. Many students are unsuccessful in the course and flunk the state examination. Upon analysis, it appears that students who are failing the exam, and the course, can be identified as early as the first marking period, yet they are given no additional help the rest of the year. Questions also develop around the issue of preparedness for Math I—how did this year's failing students achieve in the previous years?

Remedies could include:

- more instantaneous help for students who are identified as at risk for failing
- more rigorous preparatory programs and a three semester course for those who need a slower pace.

Levels of Root Cause

Root Causes can be found at any one of the following levels:

- *Incident* or *procedural level*

  Example: A fight in the cafeteria, fifth period on Wednesday.

- *Programmatic* or *process level*

  Example: There are always fights in the cafeteria, every day, at every period.

- *Systemic level*

  Example: There are fights everywhere in school.

- *External level*

Example: The whole community is fighting.

It is important not to make an "incident" into a systemic issue or to treat a true systemic issue as simply a bunch of incidents.

An administrative colleague came running into my office, very upset that the phone system that morning was completely overloaded, and he demanded that we rapidly proceed with a process to replace what he felt was an outmoded system. Not being as emotionally involved as he, I asked, "How often does this happen?" He responded to the effect that he didn't know. I asked, "Is it once a week, every day, once a month or rarely?" Again, he could not tell me. All he knew was that it was an immediate concern of his that morning. Yet, without knowing the frequency of the problem, I had no way of knowing if it was an extremely rare incident or something that was systemically wrong with our phone system. To initiate a process of replacement based upon an isolated incident would be wasteful, yet, many times incidents are treated as if they are systemic or programmatic in nature. I believe this is as true in the classroom as it is in the office.

Examples of elements at each level are:

Incident or procedural level:

- the student
- the test

- the teacher
- the incident

Programmatic level:

- instructional processes
- materials
- setting
- time
- alignment

- grouping
- scheduling
- training and staff development
- administrative procedures
- curriculumassessment

Systemic level:

- leadership
- mission
- vision
- priorities
- morale
- planning
- budget
- policies
- values/beliefs
- organizational structure

- allocation of staff
- culture
- facilities
- technology
- competencies
- collaboration
- evaluation
- history
- capacity

External level:

- family
- community
- gangs
- wealth/poverty

- health
- partnerships and supporting agencies
- the media
- youth culture

The external level is the most difficult to deal with because we do not have the ability to control it. As educators, however, we often want to point the figure of blame in this direction. I think, however, that most schools have enough to solve within their own walls before venturing out to solve the world's problems. Nevertheless, if a school desires to improve external issues, there are several strategies to follow:

♦ The ability to influence, e.g., the Great American Smoke-Out Day

♦ Proactive mechanisms, e.g., pre-schools, pre-school book bags

♦ Collaborations, e.g., with Head Start, Even Start, etc.

♦ Compensating mechanisms, e.g., remediation, extra time, etc.

There are those who believe that if we dig deeply enough, seeking cause within a system, we will nearly always end up at the system level. It is another way of saying what President Truman succinctly stated as "The Buck Stops Here." These same people will go on to say that there are usually just a few major system causes that become manifested in a wide variety of seemingly separate and differentiated symptoms. Lack of leadership and direction, for example, will result in widespread, seemingly chaotic, manifestations. On the other hand, I would not want to automatically assign cause for an incidental fight in the cafeteria, at fifth period on Wednesday, to the Superintendent or Board of Education. The most immediate roots for such an incident most likely lie within the participants and, perhaps, within those most closely responsible for their care.

Thus, although roots at the system level will no doubt cause a variety of symptoms throughout the system, there most certainly exist shallower roots that are confined to the program and incident level.

The Longitudinal Stream

The preceding discussion identified various levels within the system where causes are to be found. The concept of "levels" brings forth vertical imagery for the location of cause. But, schools are also longitudinal in nature, given that it takes thirteen years or more for a student to complete requirements for the typical high school diploma.

Those who seek root cause must therefore be aware of what, for lack of a better term, I characterize as the "longitudinal stream" of causation. An incident or program failure at the high school, for example, might be traced vertically to a systemic issue that occurred at much earlier grade levels.

> **Example**: A high school experiences a dropout rate of 30 percent between the beginning of ninth grade and the end of tenth. Although one might seek cause within the high school itself, it is more than likely that a thorough review of data will reveal that those who drop out can be identified much earlier in the systemic stream. If so, the greatest leverage for change will not necessarily be at the ninth- and tenth-grade levels—although interventions at those levels may help—but at the point where these future dropouts can first be identified.

This example also illustrates why the most effective root cause analysis processes are not limited to the study of individual buildings, grades, or classrooms, but rather are system-wide in scope.

When is a Cause a Root Cause?

In complex social systems, such as schools, it may be difficult, if not impossible, to identify a single, specific, root cause. Often, there are clusters of causal factors that each contribute to the problem. Sometimes, dissolution of any one of the casual factors is sufficient to substantially reduce or totally eliminate the problem. The following concepts provide some direction in identifying root causes or clusters of causal factors.

Ammerman[1] has identified three criteria to determine if each identified cause is a root cause or if it is a contributing cause. They are:

1. Would the problem have occurred if the cause had not been present?

    If no, then it is a root cause.

    If yes, then it is a contributing cause.

2. Will the problem reoccur as the result of the same cause if the cause is corrected or dissolved?

    If no, then it is a root cause.

---

1 Ammerman, M. (1998). The root cause analysis handbook: A simplified approach to identifying, correcting and reporting workplace errors (pp. 66–67). New York: Quality Resources.

If yes, then it is a contributing cause.

3. Will correction or dissolution of the cause lead to similar events?

If no, then it is a root cause.

If yes, then it is a contributing cause.

Other indicators that you have found the root cause are:[2]

♦ You run into a dead end asking what caused the proposed root cause.

♦ Everyone agrees that this is a root cause.

♦ The cause is logical, makes sense, and provides clarity to the problem.

♦ The cause is something that you can influence and control.

♦ If the cause is dissolved, there is realistic hope that the problem can be reduced or prevented in the future.

School improvement teams and others using root cause analysis often wonder when to stop seeking cause and make the decision that sufficient data and effort have been used to arrive at a reasonable root. This is often a judgment call that will improve with experience. Often, the lack of data and the pressures of time frustrate the effort and force it to halt at a level below the surface symptom, but perhaps not as deep as must it ultimately go. In my view, this is the reality of life in a less-than-perfect world. Using the above guides and common sense, however, teams can usually arrive at a proximate area of cause or causes that if dissolved, or reduced, will remedy or reduce the symptom. Teams, however, should not allow timidity or fear to block deeper discovery of issues that may be related to culture or deeper organizational elements.

Summary

This chapter presents the rationale for the use of root cause analysis as an effective means of "dissolving" problems within schools. Although this guide focuses on issues of student academic performance, root cause analysis is easily adapted for use in all areas of school operations.

A definition of root cause has been offered:

---

2 Adapted from a listing in Root cause analysis in health care: Tools and techniques (p. 71). (2000). Oakbrook Terrace, IL: Joint Commission on Accreditation of Healthcare Organizations.

Root Cause—*the deepest underlying cause, or causes, of positive or negative symptoms within any process that, if dissolved, would result in elimination, or substantial reduction, of the symptom.*

It is hoped that through an understanding of the concepts presented on the four modalities of root cause, the four levels where root causes can be found and the longitudinal nature of root cause analysis in schools, one can better "see" the whole of root cause analysis without becoming lost in its seeming complexity.

Finally, one has to sense, feel, and know the proper time to conclude the analysis and then move on to selection and implementation of strategies to dissolve the causes that have been laid bare. For some this may just be common sense, for others it may take a while to internalize. The fact is that the path of least resistance, jumping from problem to solution without considering cause, has been the more traditional process within schools than has been the process of pausing to examine root cause. The initial effort and changes in mindset necessary for proper root cause analysis will, however, pay rich dividends in the improvement of learning for all students.

2

Key Indicators
of Student Success

While the idea of focusing on student learning goals is simple, its implications are profound. It means turning most school improvement activities on their heads. Frequently, school improvement begins with some activity such as implementing a new curriculum. Clearly, planners want these innovations to improve student learning, but they are often unclear about what they mean by student learning, how they will measure it, and whether their actions are getting them to where they want to go. The result is a vicious cycle of doing, doing, doing, without knowing the effect on learning.

Nancy Love, *Using Data—Getting Results*

The Importance of Key Indicators

This short overview of *Key Indicators of Student Success* (KISS) is written as both a guide and as stimulation for discussion. It is hoped that it will serve to support and feed local school district capacity to improve learning for all students.

Although root cause analysis can certainly be used in a variety of contexts, many of which will be single incidents, programs, or even nonacademic issues, the most powerful use of root cause analysis in schools occurs within a systemic process of school improvement.

Having been involved in New York State's Comprehensive District Educational Planning (CDEP) process for the past six years, I have had ample opportunity to study its development, application, and impact. I have become increasingly sensitive to the importance of the selection and development of KISS to all planning processes. Key indicators make standards for students both visible and measurable. Without them, it is most difficult, if not impossible, to measure school effectiveness or attempt to improve learning.

*A **Key Indicator of Student Success** is: a student-focused measurable result that the school has the ability, desire, or need to influence and for which it is willing, or required, to be held accountable.*

Collectively, a school's Key Indicators of Student Success make a school's standards tangible in a way similar to how iron filings make a magnetic field visible.

The content of a school's key student indicators are driven by required standards established by the state or other entity, the district's own standards, and its mission, vision, values, and beliefs. Although key indicators for a military academy, parochial school, public school, or alternative school, will be similar to some degree, it would be expected that they will also vary with the differing missions and beliefs of the schools.

Key indicators, in turn, must drive both formative and summative assessments. Curriculum and instruction must be informed by, aligned with, and be responsive to all key indicators. Key indicators also supply the basic student data upon which planning is built, and that planning should drive the school system toward improved achievement of the indicators by all students. School goals should be ends-focused, rather than means-focused, and should be written in terms of KISS.

The schematic in Figure 2.1 is a graphic overview of these concepts. Although all parts in a system are linked, in the schematic, arrows have been drawn only to show what are considered to be the major linkages among the parts for the purpose of this discussion. In reality, all elements of the schematic are connected to at least some degree.

Key Indicators of Student Success are what the system is all about. Key indicators are the purpose, goals, or "end results" of the school system. All other items are strategies, tactics, inputs or means.

An essential component of stating a key indicator is to identify exactly how the indicator will be measured. In some cases this is relatively simple. Listed in Figure 2.2 (page 18) are several potential key indicators with possible means of measurement identified.

In other cases, it will be most difficult to establish how a key indicator will be measured, and, in some cases, it has taken several years to find or develop suitable measures. If the indicator is seen as important, however, this should not stop the effort. How can a school state as an objective something that it has no ability to measure? How can anyone be held accountable for its achievement?

The selection of KISS and the identification of how each will be measured stimulates much discussion, sometimes heated debate, and certainly much personal and organizational reflection. Once established and communicated, however, the indicators, and the means by which they will be measured, add great clarity not only to the school improvement and root cause analysis process, but to all processes within the school.

Figure 2.1. The Central Importance of Key Indicators of Student Success

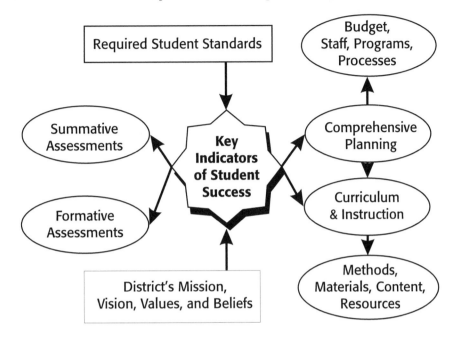

Key Indicator of Student Success = A student-focused measurable outcome that the school has the ability, desire, or need to influence and for which it is willing, or required, to be held accountable.

Key Indicators of Student Success (KISS) are the most tangible aspect of a school's standards. They are derived from both internal and external standards and the school's mission, vision, values and beliefs. Key indicators should drive both formative and summative assessment of student learning, as well as curriculum and instruction (methods, materials, content and resources). Key indicators provide the basis for the analysis of data that is essential for comprehensive planning and ongoing school improvement. Through comprehensive planning, key indicators should influence: budget, staff development and professional performance review, staffing, instructional programs, and other significant school processes. School goals should be written in terms of the key indicators.

At the end of this chapter there are two templates for use in working with key indicators. The first, the Key Indicator Template (Figure 2.12), provides a box for each key indicator as well as a box to describe how that indicator will be measured. For those who use a pareto tool to prioritize (rank or weigh) the relative importance of each indicator, smaller boxes are provided to record that information as well. The second, the Planning Template (Figure 2.13), is for use in building a planning process directly from each key indicator. This template may need to be expanded, depending upon the amount of information presented in each box, but it provides a graphic overview of the flow from identification of the key indicator through a complete data-based planning process. Examples of how this template can be used will be discussed later in this chapter.

Figure 2.2. Means for Measuring KISS

Key Indicator of Student Success	As Measured By:
Student attendance	Daily, weekly, monthly, and annual attendance records
English language competency	State assessment
	Standardized assessment
	Teacher-given grade
	Student work/portfolio
Student "engagement" in school	Participation in activities
	Student survey

The Verification Process

In nearly all aspects of root cause analysis, and in other aspects of school improvement planning, it is essential that some sort of verification process be implemented to ensure the legitimacy and reliability of what is being presented. No representative group of stakeholders, no matter how diligent or diverse, can develop the perfect product in isolation. The verification process does not ensure perfection, but does enable many more voices to contribute and to feel greater ownership in the final product.

Simply put, *verification* is the process by which a team product, such as the listing of Key Indicators of Student Success, is publicly disseminated and reviewed with the intent of using the input generated to modify the list before it becomes finalized. It is essential that all aspects of root cause analysis, and other school improvement initiatives, remain as open to all stakeholders as possible. Verification meets this need.

In working with KISS, the verification process might work in the following manner:

♦ The concept of Key Indicators of Student Success is explained to all stakeholders, and their input is solicited as to what they think are key indicators and measures.

♦ The team sorts and begins to refine a composite listing of key indicators, including their own items and concepts. The team is careful to keep the focus on student end results, rather than on means or nonstudent issues.

♦ Means for measuring each key indicator must also be identified.

- The team prioritizes its indicators using any one of a variety of paretoing techniques. This is a means of distinguishing the most important indicators from those of lesser importance.

- The team distributes its shortened list of high-priority indicators, and the means by which they are to be measured, for comment by the many stakeholder groups.

- The team takes the comments, modifies the listing and measurements as it sees fit, and passes them on to the Board of Education for final acceptance.

Because Key Indicators of Student Success will direct not only root cause analysis but also much of all else that the district does, it is essential that care be taken in the development of this essential organizational compass.

Two examples of initial efforts by school districts to identify Key Indicators of Student Success are presented, respectively, in Figures 2.3 and 2.4. In Figure 2.3, the initial list of key indicators was developed through brainstorming by a team that was coordinating a district's planning efforts. They took the additional step of dividing the indicators by grade level. Only student-focused indicators were eventually accepted, and items that were considered "means" rather than "ends" were eliminated. Class size, for example, although a measurement, is not specifically focused on student results, nor is it an "end" goal of the school. Class size is a "means" issue and, therefore, a potential strategy—not a goal. Critical indicators of student success must be student-focused, capable of being influenced by the school and issues for which the school expects to be held accountable.

Figure 2.3. Leatherhand Central School District—Listing of Potential Key Indicators of Student Success

Indicator	High School	Middle School	Elementary School
Attendance Rates	Yes	Yes	Yes
Tardiness Rates	Yes	Yes	Yes
Cut Rates	Yes	Yes	
Suspension Rates (IS/OS)	Yes	Yes	
State Testing Results	Yes	Yes	Yes
Student Grades (report cards)	Yes	Yes	Yes
Graduation Rates	Yes		

Indicator	High School	Middle School	Elementary School
Promotion Rates	Yes	Yes	
Percent "Social Promotions"	Yes	Yes	
Regents Diploma Rates	Yes		
Percent Going to College	Yes		
Percent G.E.D.	Yes		
Number of Students in Activities	Yes	Yes	Yes
Number of Students in Alternative Education	Yes		
Free/Reduced Lunch	Yes		
Number in AP/College Courses	Yes		
Accelerated Courses	Yes		
SAT Scores	Yes		
Percent on Honor Roll	Yes	Yes	
Percent Academic Ineligible	Yes		
Customer Satisfaction	Yes		
Percent Foreign Language Proficiency Exam	Yes		
Percent of Students in Pre-K	Yes		
Percent of Emergent Readers	Yes		
Physical Fitness Test	Yes	Yes	Yes
Terranova Test	Yes		
Early Literacy Profile	Yes	Yes	
Special Education Identifications	Yes	Yes	Yes

Because this was the very beginning of what was to become a long-term, data-focused school improvement planning effort, the coordinating team prioritized their listing. This ordering resulted in the most important and immediate state assessments receiving the highest priority as Key Indicators of Student Success, but this result does not always occur; many school systems develop a greater variety of key indicators.

As part of its comprehensive planning process, another school district started by listing its key indicators of student success using the outline of "multiple measures" as described by Dr. Victoria Bernhardt.[1]

Figure 2.4. Riverside CSD—Listing of Potential Key Indicators of Student Success

Category	KISS
Student Achievement	
Results of State Assessment Program—All Tests	x
Local Standardized Testing Program	x
Teacher-Given Student Grades	x
Locally-Driven Goal Areas	x
Student Demographics	
Course Enrollment	
Student Identification (gender, wealth, ethnicity, etc.)	
Program Enrollments	
School Processes	
Attendance Rates	x
Dropout Rates	x
Disciplinary Rates	x
Participation Rates	x
Tardy Rates	x
Graduation Rates	x
Diploma Rates	x
Next Step Following Graduation Rates	x
Retention Rates	x

---

1 V. Bernhardt, *Data analysis for comprehensive schoolwide improvement*, Eye On Education, 6 Depot Way West, Suite 106, Larchmont, NY 10538.

Special Education Placement Rates   x

Perceptive Data

Student Perceptions   x

Parent Perceptions

Staff Perceptions

Community Perceptions

Although all of the indicators listed in Figure 2.4 are valid measures of school performance, only those marked with an "x" are true to the definition of a Key Indicator of Student Success. The other indicators are certainly valid as sources of information but not as targets in and of themselves.

Other School Indicators

In the search for root cause, and in the improvement of schools in general, there are other indicators that are not student-focused, but rather are inputs or means that are necessary to support student learning. A partial listing of some of these other possible indicators is provided in Figure 2.5 as a means of clarifying what is, and what is not, a Key Indicator of Student Success.

Each of the indicators in Figure 2.5 provides a "window" into the school as a system, and, in its own way, adds to our knowledge about the school. None of these, however, are Key Indicators of Student Success because they are measures of means that support student learning rather than the "ends" that *are* student learning. They cannot be used as a basis for instructional goal statements. Some can, however, be used as areas of strategic leverage to improve learning.

It is a relatively easy transition to adapt the concepts mentioned above to nonacademic areas. A school district, board, or administration may, for example, want to develop a more widespread listing of school indicators of quality or efficiency. Once established, such indicators can be used in the same manner as Key Indicators of Student Success to monitor and improve nonacademic school processes such as staffing, finances, physical plant, maintenance, busing, food programs, public perceptions, etc. The focus of this text, however, remains on the use of these concepts in the pursuit of student academic achievement.

Figure 2.5. Indicators That Are Not Student-Focused

Indicator	Input That Supports Student Learning
Tax rate on true value	Community wealth
Tax rate as percentage of wealth (effort)	Budget
Per pupil expenditure	Line item expenditures
Teacher/student ratio	Class Size
Teacher turnover rates	Teacher certification
Teacher degrees held	Teacher placement on "steps"
Teacher demographics	Board of Education turnover
Leadership turnover rates	Average teacher salary
Number of support personnel	Staff absentee rates
Student demographics	Student mobility
Physical facilities (size, age, quality, suitability)	Number of library books
Computer stations per student	
School district efficiency (The degree to which inputs result in learning)	

Using Key Indicators of Student Success

Three examples follow showing how Key Indicators of Student Success can be used to drive a school improvement planning process or comprehensive school reform. A planning template for this format is provided in Figure 2.13 at the end of this chapter.

Example 1

Key Indicator:	*Student graduation rate*
Desired Ideal Condition:	100 percent of the entering ninth-grade cohort will ultimately receive a high school diploma
Present Condition:	84 percent of the entering ninth-grade cohort receives a high school diploma

Gap (Opportunity for Improvement):	■ 16 percent of the entering ninth-grade cohort does not receive a high school diploma
	  • 12 percent drop out
	  • 3 percent receive certificates
	  • 1 percent fails to graduate in the senior year

Is This a Priority Issue?	Yes!
Goal Statement:	Over the course of the next four-year period, the percentage of the students in the ninth-grade cohort who graduate with a diploma will increase from the present 84 percent to 100 percent.
Search for Root Cause:	Examine why/when/how/which students drop out Examine if some certificate students could reasonably obtain a diploma with extra time or help Examine how senior failures can be eliminated
Possible Strategies for Improvement:	Identify potential dropouts earlier Provide special attention to those so identified Provide assistance for certificate-bound students Prevent senior failures

---

Example 2

Key Indicator:	*Student failure rate— freshman class (ninth grade)*
Desired Ideal Condition:	■ 100 percent of the entering ninth-grade cohort will pass all of their courses the first time enrolled
Present Condition:	■ 52 percent of all freshman have at least one "F" final grade ■ 257 "F" grades were issued to the freshman class ■ 1.4 "F" grades were issued per student
Gap (Opportunity for Improvement):	■ 257 failing grades ■ 52 percent of students with at least one "F"
Is This a Priority Issue?:	Yes!
Goal Statement:	Over the course of the next three year period we will reduce the number of ninth-grade student failures from the present 52 percent of all freshman to 0 percent.
Search for Root Cause:	Examine why/when/how/which students fail
Selection of Strategies for Improvement:	Eliminate causes for freshman failure

---

Example 3

Key Indicator:	*Student achievement on fourth-grade state test*
Desired Ideal Condition:	■ 100 percent of all fourth-grade students will score at least a 3 on the state English Language Arts Examination
Present Condition:	■ 18 percent scored at Level 1 ■ 25 percent scored at Level 2 ■ 34 percent scored at Level 3 ■ 23 percent scored at Level 4
Gap (Opportunity for Improvement):	■ 43 percent of students score below level 3
Is This a Priority Issue:	Yes!
Goal Statement:	Over the course of the next three-year period we will reduce the number of fourth-grade students scoring below Level 3 from 43 percent to 0 percent.
Search for Root Cause:	Examine why/when/how/which students fail
Selection of Strategies for Improvement	Eliminate causes for failure

As can be seen from the above examples, goal statements are a derivative of the desired ideal condition with the addition of a timeline and starting point. Both the statement of the desired ideal condition and the goal statement clarify and quantify the concept of key indicator. Gaps can only be identified once the key indicator has been quantified. The gap is then simply the difference between what is and what is desired.

Schools are often faced with many more gaps in student performance than can be successfully dealt with at one time. It therefore is necessary to prioritize the gaps in terms of their importance and/or immediacy, with the high-priority gaps becoming the focus of the comprehensive planning and school improvement process. Once gaps are identified, and prioritized, a root cause analysis process can begin on the high-priority gaps. Goal statements are developed as targets against which the school must continually measure itself.

The presence of Key Indicators of Student Success guides those working on school improvement through what has become known as the "data swamp." It is simple to become overwhelmed at the amount of data that a typical school generates and then fail to identify the data that are important to study.

The use of the ideal condition is seen by some as setting schools up for failure because they believe the ideal is impossible to obtain. On the other hand, if less than the ideal is aimed for, what lesser percentage is acceptable? Selecting either option brings a unique set of issues. No matter which option is taken by a school, however, it is important that all understand why that particular option has been chosen and the special meaning it has for that school.

Means vs. Ends—Student Results-Focused Goal Statements

During the course of the CDEP pilot we have found that many districts have had a difficult time adapting to the new "culture" of systems thinking and results-focused planning. One of the sticking points has been the inability to differentiate between "means" and "ends." It is my firm belief that all school goals should be student-centered and expressed in terms of student learning objectives. Schools are for learning. Goals must be "ends-focused" and not statements of how we hope to get there. The "how we get there" plans are the strategies, the tactics, and the means we use to achieve our ends.

Some Data on Goal Statements

Seventy-two school district plans were reviewed to study the quality of goal statements. Eleven districts had no goal statements focused on student achievement (15 percent); 27 districts had some student-focused goal statements (38 percent); and 34 districts had all goals focused on student achievement (47 percent). Of the 310 goal statements from the 72 districts, 117 (38 percent) focused on something other than student learning.

Examples of "Means-Focused" Goal Statements

M500   Continue to implement curriculum cycle.

M501   Communicate to all employees about the contribution and importance to student learning of what they do.

M502   Communicate to parents, students, and the community.

M503   District team needs to finalize, get approval of, and implement exit outcomes.

M504   To explore/study the availability of math remediation for students transitioning from middle to high school.

M505   To increase the breadth and diversity of curricular offerings to enable students to experience every available avenue of learning.

Examples of "Ends-Focused" Goal Statements

E001   To improve percentage passing Math I examination.

E002   To improve percentage passing Global Studies examination.

E003   To lower dropout rate.

E004   To continue improvement of elementary success on state tests.

E005   Continue to improve student achievement.

E039   80 percent or higher of all students will score at level 3 or 4 in the new ELA state assessment (K-8)

E041   Increase by 3 percent to 5 percent the number of Grade 4 students who score at or above the ELA (English Language Arts) SRP (State Reference Point) relative to the 1998–99 Grade 3 comparative baseline.

E067   90 percent of the students will be able to demonstrate reading mastery by the end of grade 3.

Although the goal statements presented in the immediately preceding example are focused on ends, some are much better than others. Statement E005 is so general, for example, as to be almost meaningless in guiding the work of school improvement or improved student learning.

Complete ends-focused goal statements need to contain the following elements:

- focused on student learning

- contain a specific target for achievement compared to the present

- provide a time frame for achievement of the target

Examples of Complete "Ends-Focused" Goal Statements

The Banneker Goals—included in the Cooperative Agreement between the National Science Foundation and the Omaha Public Schools—provide a good example. Two of them follow:

1. The number and/or percentage (by grade level) of underrepresented minority eighth-grade students in the Omaha Public Schools who successfully complete Algebra I shall increase from 59, or 6 percent, of minority eighth graders to 186, or 20 percent, of the total minority eighth graders over the five-year period of this award.

2. The number and/or percentage (by grade level) of underrepresented minority ninth-grade students in the Omaha Public Schools who successfully complete Algebra I shall increase from 115, or 9 percent, of minority ninth graders to 435, or 35 percent, of the total minority ninth graders over the five-year period of this award.

Key Indicators and Goal Statements

There is a direct relationship between the identification of a school's Key Indicators of Student Success and the development of goal statements. Figure 2.6 attempts to graphically illustrate not only that relationship, but the sequence of steps used within the context of a school improvement planning process. Although the model used is New York's Comprehensive District Educational Planning (CDEP) model, most any required state, or other school improvement planning model, could be substituted for it.

Figure 2.6. New York's Comprehensive District Educational Planning: Importance of Key Indicators and Root Cause Analysis

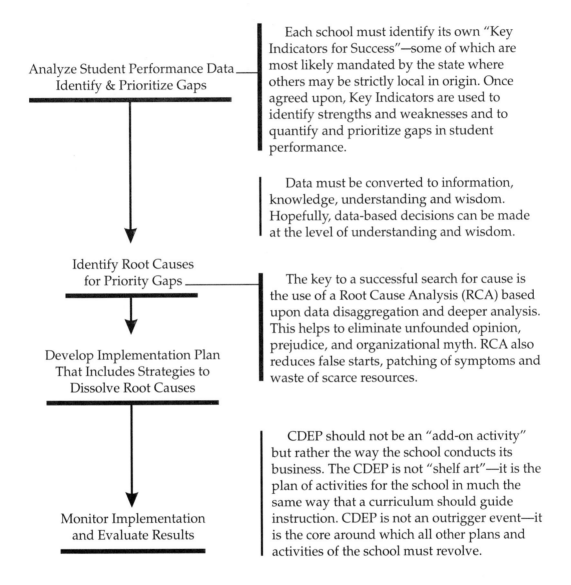

Analyze Student Performance Data
Identify & Prioritize Gaps

Each school must identify its own "Key Indicators for Success"—some of which are most likely mandated by the state where others may be strictly local in origin. Once agreed upon, Key Indicators are used to identify strengths and weaknesses and to quantify and prioritize gaps in student performance.

Data must be converted to information, knowledge, understanding and wisdom. Hopefully, data-based decisions can be made at the level of understanding and wisdom.

Identify Root Causes
for Priority Gaps

The key to a successful search for cause is the use of a Root Cause Analysis (RCA) based upon data disaggregation and deeper analysis. This helps to eliminate unfounded opinion, prejudice, and organizational myth. RCA also reduces false starts, patching of symptoms and waste of scarce resources.

Develop Implementation Plan
That Includes Strategies to
Dissolve Root Causes

CDEP should not be an "add-on activity" but rather the way the school conducts its business. The CDEP is not "shelf art"—it is the plan of activities for the school in much the same way that a curriculum should guide instruction. CDEP is not an outrigger event—it is the core around which all other plans and activities of the school must revolve.

Monitor Implementation
and Evaluate Results

Flowchart graphically illustrates Comprehensive District Educational Planning (CDEP) as a four-step process. Its original format was six steps.

Comments developed by Dr. Preuss for use with, and in support of, New York's Comprehensive District Educational Planning process.

The identification of priority *Key Indicators of Student Success* (KISS) is an essential first step. A school then needs to clarify and state its expectations in terms of a *Desired Ideal Condition*. The school's present condition is then compared with its expectation through the use of data. No doubt, *Gaps* will be identified. Within CDEP, such *Gaps* are prioritized, and the most important become the primary focus of the plan. Using both the *Desired Ideal Condition*, and the measurement of the *Gap*, an "ends-focused" *Goal Statement* is developed.

At this point, the bulk of the planning process begins with the *Search for Root Cause, Selection of Strategies*, development of the *Action Plan* and the implementation of ongoing *Monitoring and Evaluation*.

It is not my purpose at this point to go into a detailed discussion of each of these steps, but rather to show how *Key Indicators of Student Success* and *Goal Statements* are essential to whatever school improvement or planning process is used.

Without selecting specific *Key Indicators of Student Success* the process can soon become bogged down in a morass of data guided by whim, anecdote, or chance rather than by purpose. Without stating goals clearly in terms of student success indicators, it is easy to get caught in the trap of focusing on means rather than ends.

Key Indicators of Student Success and "ends-focused" *Goal Statements* are essential for the monitoring and evaluation of results. Figure 2.7 provides a completed planning template showing these relationships.

Figure 2.7. Key Indicators and Goal Statements

Planning Process	*Example of how a Key Indicator Drives the Planning Process*

Key Indicator of Student Success ———— Percentage of Academic Diploma Graduates

↓

Desired Ideal Condition ———— 100% of Students will graduate with an Academic Diploma

↓

Present Condition ———— 1995 = 45%   1996 = 48%   1997 = 44%
1998 = 52%   1999 = 55%   2000 = 60%

↓

Gap ———— Last year and the best year, gap = 40% Over the last six years gap averaged 51%

↓

Is This a Priority Issue? ———— *YES!*

↓

Goal Statement ———— **100% of Graduates will receive an Academic Diploma by the graduating Class of 2005 and thereafter.**

↓

Search for Root Cause ———— Data Analysis to seek who is not obtaining a regents diploma, and why they are not.

↓

Selection of Strategies ———— Strategies are focused on dissolving the root causes, not on patching the system—or student.

↓

Development and Implementation of Action Plan ———— Who will do what, by when, with what resources, to implement the strategies.

↓

Monitoring and Evaluation ———— Ongoing - How are we doing? Monitor both implementation of strategies and goal.

Terminology

Unfortunately, the educational profession does not have clear and unambiguous terminology to describe its processes, procedures, or content. This causes continual problems in communication and application of concepts. We continually fight the battle of semantics.

The term *Key Indicator of Student Success* (KISS) for example, is often referred to as any one of the following:

- Student Success Indicator
- Outcome Indicator
- Target
- Indicator of Success
- Measure of Success
- Outcome

- Student Performance Indicator
- Benchmark
- Success Indicator
- Key Measure
- Achievement Indicator
- Goal

Each of these terms, in turn, has its own series of multiple meanings depending upon who is doing the writing.

Perhaps it is hopeless to strive for uniform usage across the realm of education, but it is necessary within a single context (such as a school) or process (such as school improvement planning), to develop as much consistency and uniformity as possible. We can then not only communicate more effectively within our own context but can also "translate" from the terminology used in other sources or contexts to the terms we are using in our own.

A glossary is provided in Chapter 7 of this guide to explain the meanings behind the various terms used in this text and to assist districts in arriving at common usage, should they decide to follow this model.

One Final Example: The Moose River CSD

The following discussion illustrates the development of Key Indicators of Student Success with an example taken from the field—The Moose River Central School District (CSD). Although this example is not perfect, it does illustrate the concepts discussed earlier. The products shared were the result of a half-day planning session. *Facilitator's Comments* provide a general overview, and the *Agenda* (Figure 2.9) details the process used during the three-hour session.

The listing of key indicators is weighted and provides much food for thought in revealing this district's attempt at verbalizing its most important issues at this time. Finally, preliminary means of measuring each weighted key indicator were identified. The next phase of this process included verification of what the team had done by all district stakeholders and further clarifying the language and intent of each item.

It is obvious that some key indicators are harder to measure than others. This did not stop this team, however, from insisting on stating what they thought were the most important goals of their school. A search for more valid and reliable measures will continue for these items.

A Key Indicators Discovery Process—Half Day

The following discussion contains examples of work produced during a half-day facilitated session at the Moose River CSD. The products of the day—an Initial Listing of Key Indicators of Student Success as Pareotoed (Figure 2.10) and Key Indicators and Preliminary Listing of Measures (Figure 2.11)—were shared with all key stakeholder groups for comment and revision. The initial committee was then to make an updated listing for participants as a basis for continuation of the process. Coincidentally, data was gathered using the measures identified. Where data was absent, measures had to be instituted to gather the information.

Facilitator's Comments

The Facilitator's Comments, below, were shared with the team along with the product pages (Figures 2.10 and 2.11). The comments are based upon data from the figures that follow (Figures 2.8 to 2.11).

> *The Process Used* is best described by the flow chart following this page [see Agenda, Figure 2.9]. Weighting was on a 1, 3, 5 scale with each item weighted by each of the seven participants. Five points were to be awarded to an item if it was immediate and significant, three points if it was less immediate and one point if it was perceived as a "back burner" issue. The weights reported are averages since some items were weighted by all seven members of the group while a few others were weighted by six.
>
> Two issues seemed to surface in a variety of ways:
>
>> Items 5, 10, and 16/4 all deal with issues of success following graduation and comparability of Moose River graduates with cohorts from similar school districts. In fact items 4 and 16 were combined because the group agreed that they were so similar in thrust. Areas identified included:
>>
>> • ability of students to "stay the course at college or employment" following graduation

- comparability of Moose River CSD grading system with other standards

In fact these three items ranked near the top of the paretoing.

Items 1, part of 3, 10, 15, and 18 all deal with aspects of student behavior and attitude. Even item 14, which was placed in the "parking lot" has some of its roots in the question of how well the district serves students who are not successful in school. There appears to this facilitator, an underlying theme of concern over student actions and their interaction with each other and adults.

Item 3 is different enough to be commented on separately. It is almost a summary of all that is being said in each of the other key indicators and as such is a type of "umbrella" under which all of the others can fit, yet it deserves remaining as an item in its own right.

On the following pages the items will be shown with Pareto "bar charts" which provide a visual picture of the weighting. The Pareto concept is based on the idea that 80 percent of your success will come from 20 percent of the items identified. The weighting process is designed to identify that top 20 percent which should become the focus of school improvement efforts. Examples of the Pareto concept include such things as "80 percent of speeding come from 20 percent of the drivers, or 80 percent of absences come from 20 percent of students.

These Paretoed Items must be "verified" by all other stakeholder groups. This process includes the sharing of the identified Key Indicators of Student Success and the weighting and seeking feedback for items missed or items in need of clarification.

In some instances the small groups had established various rates for some of the key indicators. These have been left out of the primary documents but are reported later on for future use in developing goal statements.

A final step in our work was to attempt to identify "measures" or sources of data that could be used to quantify each of the key indicators. These are listed on the final pages of this summary. Stakeholders should also be asked for their ideas as to the "measures" to be used for each of these items.

Figure 2.8. Moose River CSD—Key Indicators of Student Success as Initially Identified

Item Number	Item	Paretoed Weight
1	Student positive self-esteem	3
2	Student perceptions of school experience[1]	2.4
3	Students as effective and productive citizens with attainable and marketable skills, personal attributes to deal with others, adaptability	5
5	Student success following school (employment/higher education)	4
6	Student performance on standardized assessments (New York State and others)	5
7	Student dropout rate	1
9	Student physical fitness	1.9
10	Student social/emotional maturity in comparison to peers from other areas (related to # 5, above)	4.7
11	Student attendance rate	2
13	Student diploma graduation rate	3.3
15	Student disciplinary referral rate	2
16/4	Student abilities as compared with students elsewhere[2]	5
17	Student computer literacy	1.8
18	Student positive "attitude" of "respect," as evidenced by lack of vandalism, positive interpersonal interactions with adults and peers	4

Items placed in "parking lot" for future discussion as strategies because they are either "means" rather than "ends" or they are greater key indicators of organizational success than student success.

8	Sufficiency of nonsport extracurricular activities	NA
12	Sufficiency of parent/teacher direct contact	NA
14	Are we "meeting needs" of students "failing" in school—disciplinary, dropouts, programmatic interventions	NA

Process: The 18 items above were developed in response to the following "Essential Question:"

> Given the many realities of today's Moose River CSD context, what are the *Key Indicators of Student Success* that we should use to indicate our district's effectiveness?

[1] Includes: teachers, sports, overall education, academic subjects, etc.
[2] Here we combined two items that were very similar—see facilitator's commentary.

Figure 2.9. Moose River CSD Half Day—Agenda

Introduction and Overview of the Task and Expected Products	Identification of Initial Listing of Key Indicators of Student Success and Possible Means of Measurement	10 minutes
↓		
Review of Concept of Key Indicators of Student Success	Importance, Definition, Examples, Transitioning from Key Indicators to Goal Statements	20 minutes
↓		
Two Small Groups Identification of Most Important Ten Key Indicators	5 Minutes Individual Reflection 20 Minutes Sharing 5 Minutes Selection of Most Important Writing Out—Newsprint	30 minutes
↓		
Small Group Reports Out and a Single Listing of Key Indicators is Developed	Reporting Out—Newsprint Discussion—Clarification Selection	30 minutes
↓		
Paretoing of Key Indicators	Weighting of Each Key Indicators (5–3–1)Looking at DistributionSelecting Primary Key Indicators	30 minutes
↓		
Identification of Key Measures	What Essential Measures Will Be Used to Assess Each Key Indicator (Level 1)	30 minutes
↓		
Summary	Review of Products in Line with Goals for the Session Next Steps	10 minutes

The Essential Question used: Given the many realities of today's Moose River CSD context—what are the Key Indicators of Student Success that we should use to measure our district's effectiveness?

Figure 2.10. Moose River CSD—Initial Listing of Key Indicators of Student Success as Paretoed

Scale		1	2	3	4	5	
Item #							Weight

Item #		Weight
3	Students as effective and productive with attainable and marketable skills, personal attributes to deal with others and adaptability	5
6	Student performance on Standard Assessments (State and Others)	5
16/4	Student abilities as Compared to Students Elsewhere	5
10	Student social/emotional maturity in comparison to peers from other area	4.7
18	Student positive "attitude" and "respect" as evidenced by lack of vandalism, positive interpersonal interactions with adults and peers	4
5	Student success following school (employment/ higher education)	4
13	Student Diploma Graduation Rate	3.3
1	Student Positive Self-Esteem	3
2	Student Perception of School Experiences	2.4
11	Student Attendance Rate	2
15	Student Disciplinary Referral Rate	2
9	Student Physical Fitness	1.9
17	Student Computer Literacy	1.8
7	Student Drop-Out Rate	1

The three divisions by shading are arbitrary but designed to convey the concept that there are indeed groupings of more important items and items of lesser importance.

Figure 2.11. Moose River CSD—Key Indicators and Preliminary Listing of Measures

Item No.	Key Indicators of Student Success	As Measured By
3	Students as effective and productive citizens with attainable and marketable skills, personal attributes to deal with others, and adaptability	Individual Career Portfolios Disciplinary Referrals Tardiness & Cuts Participation In Activities Graduate Survey
6	Student performance on Standardized Assessments (State and Others)	Grade 4 NYS ELA & Math Tests Grade 8 NYS ELA & Math Tests Grade 8 NYS Social Studies Test Terra Nova Tests in Grades 2, 3, 5, 6, 7 Grade 8 New York State Science Exam All New York State Regents Exams
16/4	Student Abilities as Compared to Students Elsewhere	Benchmarking with comparable schools Survey of Staff Perceptions Over Time
10	Student social/emotional maturity in comparison to peers from other area	Observation of students over time T.A.P. Survey
18	Student positive "attitude" and "respect" as evidenced by lack of vandalism, positive interpersonal interactions with adults and peers	Disciplinary Referrals Annual Vandalism Accounting Perceptions of Staff
5	Student Success following school (employment/ higher education)	Graduate Follow-Up Survey Compare to Career Portfolio
13	Student Diploma Graduation rate	Ninth-Grade Cohort Graduation Rate
1	Student Positive Self-Esteem	Peer Mediation/Conflict Resolution (#'s trained and degree used) T.A.P. and Other Student Surveys
2	Student Perception of School Experiences	Survey of Graduates Use Focus Groups Read bathroom walls
11	Student Attendance Rate	Attendance and Tardy Rate for both school and individual classes
15	Student Disciplinary Referral Rate	Assess disciplinary records: who/what/when/where/class

9	Student Physical Fitness	Presidential Physical Fitness Test P.E. Class Assessments
17	Student Computer Literacy	Keyboarding Skill Assessment in Seventh Grade Examine computer work required across grade levels and courses
7	Student Drop-Out Rate	Attendance and Enrollment Data by Cohort

Templates

Figure 2.12. Key Indicator Template

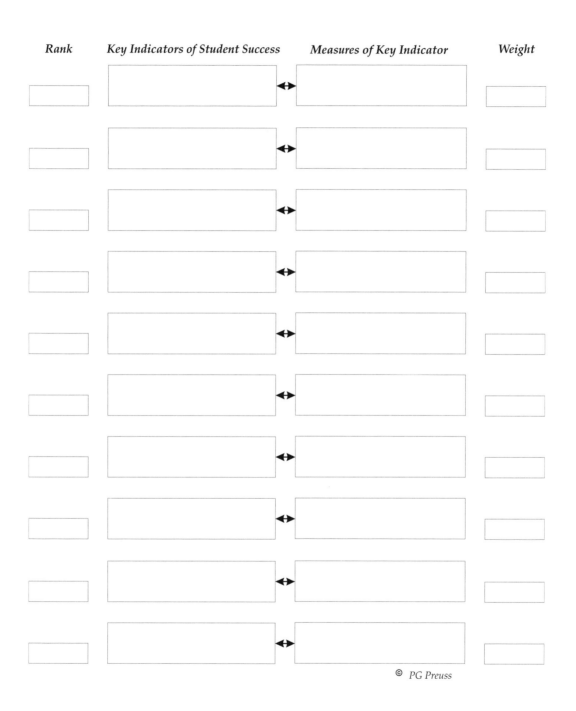

Rank   *Key Indicators of Student Success*   *Measures of Key Indicator*   *Weight*

© *PG Preuss*

Figure 2.13. Planning Template

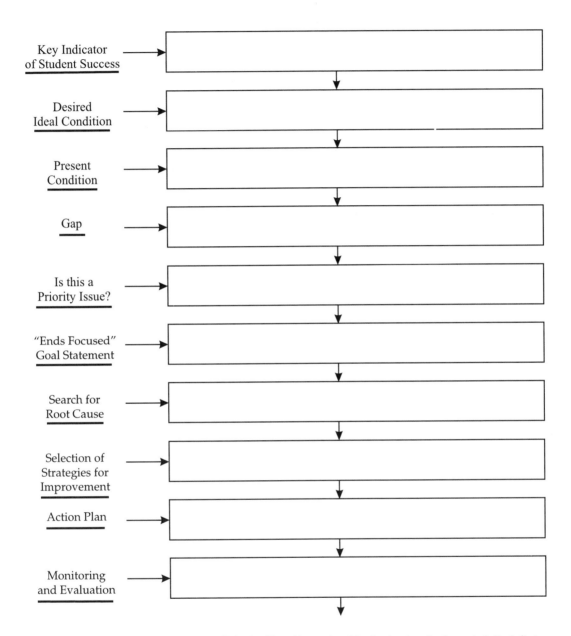

This template may be copied and used as a type of "shorthand" graphic overview of the planning stemming from a single Key Indicator of Student Success. ©PG Preuss

Summary

This chapter explored the central importance of Key Indicators of Student Success.

A **Key Indicator of Student Success** is: a student-focused measurable end result that the school has the ability, desire, or need to influence and for which it is willing, or required, to be held accountable.

Key indicators are directly related to goal statements and are therefore fundamentally necessary for root cause analysis.

Ends-focused goal statements must: be focused on student learning results, contain a specific target for achievement, and provide a time frame for reaching the target.

All work by the school improvement or planning team must be "verified" by all other stakeholder groups. This is particularly true for the development of Key Indicators of Student Success, goal statements, and root cause analysis.

It is relatively easy to confuse a focus on means with focusing on student results. Means, such as staff development, are not ends in and of themselves—they are a means to improve student learning. Key indicators and goal statements must focus on ends rather than means.

A variety of examples and schematics and templates have been provided to support the development and use of these concepts.

3

Root Cause Processes

Frequently, people in organizations persist in attacking symptoms rather than problem sources. Unfortunately, far too often, existing problem-solving methodologies barely probe below the surface. Linear, single-source cause and effect models are sufficient if one is working on a simple, single-source issue, but these models are ineffective when it comes to dealing with complex systematic problems. Thus, the root causes of the problems persist, undisturbed, to feed the symptoms and grow.

Dr. Jack L. Oxenrider, *Creative Root Cause Analysis: Team Problem Solving*

Observations and Suggested Remedies

The following observations and suggested remedies have emerged from many hours of work in helping schools use data to improve learning for all students:

♦ *Observation*: Until recently, most schools did not use data in a systematic way to improve student learning. Most often, schools moved from problem to solution without investigating data for root cause.

Remedy: Root Cause Analysis (RCA) offers a pause between problem identification and solution that allows for reflection and focusing on the issues of causation. Proper solutions must be aimed at causation, not at symptoms. Data is essential for informing reflections and for verification of opinions. RCA provides a structured problem-solving process that will lead to fundamental issues of causation within the school. By dissolving causes, symptoms will dissipate.

♦ *Observation*: Most schools find that their newly found need for data exceeds both their organizational capacity and culture.

Remedy: School infrastructure and culture need to grow in the direction of greater capacity to properly store, retrieve, analyze, and use data in all areas of decision making. This infrastructure is best located within the school district. Where this is not possible, outside agencies, such as regional school support centers, vendors, or other contractors, should be sought to provide the service. Cultural change can be effected best through committed leadership and perseverance in bringing it about.

♦ *Observation*: Many educators are not "schooled" in the proper use of data and find that they have a certain level of personal discomfort with it. A few have an outright aversion to it.

Remedy: Proper training in the use of data is best embedded in its practical use to improve learning from the classroom to the district levels. The use of data-based decision making should become the natural process that the school uses to go about its daily business. Teams, committees, leadership groups, and individual staff should become comfortable in asking the questions of data that will lead to cause. Administrative support and modeling is essential. Data must be used to seek cause, not blame. High levels of trust and low levels of fear enhance the ability to use data.

♦ *Observation*: There is a difference between "back room" data that is messy and that is used in the exploratory phases, and "presentation" data that must be clear and to the point when used to communicate to stakeholder groups.

Remedy: Data that is presented should be the distillation of much supporting data and should be in a form that is both easily understood and focused. A separate text could be written on this subject alone. Frequently, data presentation is messy, complicated, overly detailed, formatted differently, and forces the audience to struggle with its structure rather than with its meaning. Although data in its working stages may be all of these things, data for presentation must be clear, concise, and focused on its meaning for decision making.

♦ *Observation*: Schools must move to a point where data about student learning is treated as seriously, and monitored as thoroughly, as we now treat data that implicate dollar ($) amounts.

Remedy: Schools already have systems for processing a special type of data—data with a "$." Every school has a business office of some sort. Every nickel and dime is accounted for and then, often annually, audited by an independent firm whose report is made public. Few schools have an equally vast network of account clerks and data analysts whose function is to keep account of student learning. Yet, what business are we, as educators, in? Schools seeking to improve learning for all students must take seriously the importance of keeping and analyzing data about student learning, and must assign resources to the task.

♦ *Observation*: Data must be converted to information, knowledge and wisdom (Ackoff). This is best done through shared analysis, contemplation, and reflection.

Remedy: Data should become the agenda for faculty and staff discussions about improvement of learning. Data needs to be analyzed with other data to create information. Most single data sets are not all that helpful. It is only when multiple data sets are combined and analyzed that true information about the system is developed. As more information is developed, knowledge about the system expands. With ever increasing knowledge, and the ability to compare that knowledge to the knowledge generated by other systems, decisions can be made with much greater wisdom. This results in better utilization of resources such as staff time, training, and district dollars.

♦ *Observation*: Many have difficulty "seeing" what data is "showing" and then identifying possible paths for further study.

Remedy: For those who are "data challenged," it is important that a structured consistent approach to the use of data be used. As the approach is used more often, and with increasing skill, the ability to see what data is saying will improve. In the beginning, trained facilitation may be necessary to assist teams in looking at data and in identifying all that it is showing. Ultimately, however, data analysis must become an intrinsic capacity of both the school system and each of its members.

♦ *Observation*: Schools have not learned effective tools to conduct root cause analysis.

Remedy: In the following pages, a variety of root cause analysis processes are presented. The skills associated with each of these processes should become part of every educator's "toolkit" of reflective practices. RCA must become a way of thinking, from the classroom to the principal's office, to that of the superintendent and Board of Education.

Obviously, these remedies cannot all be implemented overnight. However, schools that are serious about improving achievement for all students must take steady incremental steps to continually improve their capacity to use data in arriving at sound decisions through the discovery of root causes for both successes and failures.

Root Cause Processes

The processes and tools that follow have been specifically developed for use in schools at the "whole system" level. They are also appropriate for use at the incident and program or process levels, but with the understanding that the most comprehensive search for root cause will encompass the whole of the system.

The first process deals with the concept of *"Questioning Data."* It was developed by the author as an outcome of a two-day root cause analysis workshop where the various elements of the process came together to form a very useful whole.

The second process, *The Diagnostic Tree*, has been developed for use in schools from a variety of similar approaches in other fields. These similar processes are identified by a variety of names: "why tree," "fault tree," "failure tree," and "logic tree;" however, they all contain similar elements that, when adapted to the context of public schools, provide a useful tool for seeking cause for student failure.

A third process, *The Team Discovery Process*, is best used within the context of a small team that has high expertise in the area being investigated. The initial team product must then be distributed to all important stakeholder groups to verify its validity.

The *Five Whys* is a traditional process of seeking cause and provides a sound model for digging deeply to find fundamental rather than superficial causes.

The final process, *Force Field Analysis*, can be used as a tool for both focusing discussion and presenting information to stakeholder groups.

Each of these processes combine the elements of informed professional judgment with analysis of data. A variety of templates are provided in schematic or outline format for each.

The Importance of Facilitation

When a district begins the process of formal root cause analysis, trained facilitation is essential for success. As the organization learns and becomes increasingly skilled, the need for specialized facilitation will decrease, hopefully to the point where root cause analysis is so embedded in organizational daily work that nearly all staff will become capable of conducting root cause processes.

In the beginning, however, it is wise to invest in the services of a person not only trained in facilitation, but one thoroughly familiar with the concept and tools of root cause analysis. There are several options for identifying a facilitator.

The first is to use someone from within the district. Although it is perhaps the least expensive of the options, it often comes with the largest list of inhibitors and the larger long-term cost. A primary issue is that of the potential hidden agenda brought by the in-house facilitator. While functioning as facilitator of the root cause process, the person should not advance their own ideas. This can sometime mute a person important to the investigation, or , if the facilitator contributes substantially to the search, it may often arrive at a predetermined end.

A second option is to seek professional consultant facilitation from outside of the system. Though frequently more costly, the consultant can bring to the process a wide variety and depth of skill without an agenda. It is also much easier for the consultant to remain neutral and to challenge the whole of the group when it needs to be challenged. Inhibitors may include the consultant's lack of knowledge about schools, their cultures, and specific knowledge regarding the issues under consideration. The ideal consultant is one skilled in facilitation and root cause analysis, and having deep knowledge of schools and school issues.

A third option is to seek consultant help from an educational regional support service. In different states they go by different names such as "Intermediate School District" and "Board of Cooperative Educational Services" (BOCES). Sometimes, universities have faculty or staff who serve as consultants as part of their duties. Larger teacher centers, principal centers, and other educational support programs often have staff trained and assigned to assist school districts.

Each of the following processes assumes the presence of a competent facilitator skilled in the processes of root cause analysis.

A Brief Word about Paretoing

In the next several sections the term "pareto" or "paretoing" will be used to describe the process of assigning importance or "weight" to items. The concept of pareto is that 80 percent of the result comes from 20 percent of the factors. For example, 80 percent of speeding is committed by 20 percent of the drivers, or 80 percent of school absences are made by 20 percent of the students. The purpose of paretoing items is to identify what the group thinks are the 20 percent, or the most immediate and important issues contributing to the cause.

The Questioning Data Process

The *Questioning Data Process* begins with focus upon a single set of data. Most often this is what is called a "Level One Data Set." Although this can be any data set, it is most often a data set associated with one of the school's key indicators of student success. Level One data is usually not disaggregated but presents an overview of results for the whole cohort of students being discussed. Typically, summary reports generated by standardized testing, student grading, attendance, discipline, and other processes all are Level One data.

The Questioning Data Process consists of two basic questioning steps that are reiterated, using ever more detailed data sets, until root causes are found.

Step 1:   Ask: "What do you see in this data set?"

Step 2:   Ask: "What questions do you have about what you see?"

Frequent use of this tool has demonstrated the need to maintain process discipline. Participants very quickly want to jump from observation to questioning. Without proper observation, important details in the data may be skipped over or ignored. It is suggested that the facilitator use the following guidelines to properly implement this tool.

Facilitator Guidelines

1. Present the data set—ensure that everyone understands its format and the content that it contains.

2. If the group is larger than six, divide the group into subgroups no larger than six. A group of 26 people, for example, should be divided into four groups of five and one group of six.

3. Ask each person to study the data set individually and to record his or her answers to the question: "What do I see in this data set?" Depending upon the data set, this may take between five and ten minutes. Ask the members of the whole group to hold back from thinking of questions at this time. This is often difficult for them to do.

4. After five or ten minutes, ask each of the subgroups to assemble and to share and discuss the individual responses. The task of each subgroup is to select five things that they "see" in the data to share with the whole group. This can take 10 to 20 minutes, and the facilitator should maintain contact with each of the subgroups in order to sense the proper timing.

5. Each of the subgroups reports out one of their five items in turn. The facilitator should appoint a recorder to place these items on newsprint or some other medium. The use of a recorder is suggested to free the facilitator to focus on the process rather than on writing.

6. This process will repeat itself with each of the groups in turn until all new items are reported out and recorded. With five groups reporting, it is possible to have 25 items listed. This seldom happens

because there is typically duplication, and a listing of eight to ten separate items is the norm. Depending on the number of groups reporting out, this can take from 10 to 20 minutes.

7. Although the facilitator should not usually get involved in content issues—content is owned by the group—it is appropriate at this time for the facilitator to challenge the group to ensure that as many insights into the data are identified as possible. The facilitator may ask the whole group: "Does anyone have a burning issue that has not been recorded so far?" The facilitator may ask the group if they have considered an issue that she has seen that has not been up on the board. The point is to squeeze the process in this step for as many important issues as are possible to produce.

8. In order to focus the discussion further, the facilitator asks which six of these items are the most important. The group may arrive at this through some sort of consensus or through a process of weighted voting, such as a pareto process. With less than 10 items, this will take less than ten minutes to accomplish. It is OK if the group feels that only three items, instead of six, are important enough to investigate further. If they strongly feel the need to investigate more than six, that is OK too, but see if some of the items can be merged.

9. Once the most important items have been identified, the facilitator asks the second question: "What questions do you have about what we have seen in the data?" Again, time is provided for individual reflection and thought.

   This is slightly more complex than processing the first question because individuals are now dealing with six items instead of a single data set. It is possible to assign a different item to each of six groups, but only at the risk of losing the unreported questions on that item from people in other groups. A good facilitator should be able to juggle the six items coming from all the groups, although this will take more time.

10. Once again, the individuals report back to their small subgroup and exchange the questions that they have on each item. The subgroup is assigned the task of presenting no more than two questions on each of the six items.

   In this way, if all the five subgroups respond with two questions on each of the six items, the final product will be 10 questions on each of six items for a total of 60 questions. Again, although this is possible, it very rarely happens. One often finds duplicate questions among the subgroups, and five questions on each item is more typical.

11. Once again, the subgroups report back to the larger group, and the questions are recorded on newsprint or other media. It might prove helpful if six sheets were used—one for each of the six issues identified in step 8.

   In a manner similar to that taken in step 7, the facilitator should challenge the group to ensure that all important questions are up on the board.

12. Finally, the facilitator asks the group to identify the three most important questions they have regarding each of the six issues. This can be achieved through consensus paretoing.

The group now has identified six crucial issues contained within the data set and has selected three major questions for each—a total of 18 questions. These questions will serve as guides for digging more deeply into the data. The six crucial issues and questions for each should be shared with stakeholder groups for verification and information.

Example 1: Applying the Questioning Data Process to Student Failure Rates

The Genny Eric High School Grading Report (see Figure 3.1) is used below to demonstrate how the *Questioning Data Process* works in context. It is used to monitor the following Key Indicators of Student Success:

- ◆ Percentage of students passing all courses
- ◆ Percentage of students achieving honor roll status
- ◆ Percentage of students on endangered and critical listings

The June Grading Report for the Genny Eric High School was distributed and presented to a group of 30 trainees at a root cause training session. After its format and content were made clear, the facilitator moved through steps 2 to 8.

Figure 3.1. The Genny Eric High School
Grading Report—June—Final Marks

The following data has been obtained from our final grading report for this school year:

	Freshman	Sophomore	Junior	Senior	Total	Percent
Enrollment	184	204	210	204	802	
High Honor Roll	24	24	24	44	116	14%
Honor Roll	18	20	22	30	90	11%
Total	42	44	46	74	206	26%
Percent of Class	23%	22%	22%	36%		
Endangered List	28	31	29	17	105	13%
Critical List	43	25	25	17	110	14%
Total of Class	71	56	54	34	215	27%
Percent of Class	39%	27%	26%	17%		
Number of Failing Students	96	95	100	58	349	44%
Percent of Class	52%	47%	48%	28%		
Failed 1 Course	36	42	55	34	167	21%
Failed 2 Courses	14	25	31	12	82	10%
Failed 3 Courses	18	16	10	6	50	6%
Failed 4 Courses	10	4	2	4	20	3%
Failed 5 Courses	11	4	2	1	18	2%
Failed 6 Courses	5	2	1	8	1%	
Failed 7 Courses	2	2	4	.5%		
Number of Failing Grades	257	202	165	103	727	

Critical List = students with final average below 65.

Endangered List = students with final average between 65 and 69.9

Honor Roll = students with an average between 85 and 89.9

High Honor Roll = students with an average of 90 or above.

The following six major items were identified as being "seen" in the data:

1. 52 percent of freshman failed

2. Seniors accounted for fewer failures

3. Over 12 percent of all students failed three or more subjects

4. The high school failure rate is 44 percent

5. 39 percent of freshman are on critical and endangered lists

6. 23 percent of freshman are on honor roll

These six are obviously not all the issues that can be seen, but for this group, they were the most important. In other training sessions, using this same Genny Eric data set, it is interesting to note the diversity of what different groups see, and, every once in a while, something is seen that has not been identified before.

The process now moves on to the second phase: "What questions do we have about what we see?" (steps 9 to 12).

This same training group came up with the following questions in step 12:

- 52 percent of freshman failed

  - Who are the failing freshmen?

  - What subjects did they fail?

  - Why did they fail the subject?

- Seniors accounted for fewer failures

  - Is this normal for us—for other schools?

  - What has been the dropout rate?

  - Why?

- Over 12 percent of all students failed three or more subjects

  - What are the courses most often failed?

  - What are the reasons for the failures?

  - What do these students think about why they failed?

- The high school failure rate is 44 percent

  - Is this normal for us? for other schools?

  - Who are these students?

  - Where and why are they failing?

- 39 percent of freshman are on critical and endangered lists

  - Who are these students?

- What support programs are they in, or have they been in?
- What is the relationship to discipline and attendance?
- ◆ 26 percent of freshman are on honor roll
  - Is this normal for us—for other schools?
  - Who is, and who is not, on honor roll?
  - What other factors does honor roll relate too?

For those who enjoy working with schematics, all of this information is contained in Figure 3.2. A blank template of this format (see Figure 3.21), along with an outline format (see Figure 3.22), is located at the end of the chapter for those who see advantages in using it. Often, a schematic is a simple way to define relationships and share a good deal of information on a single page.

Figure 3.2. Questioning Data Schematic

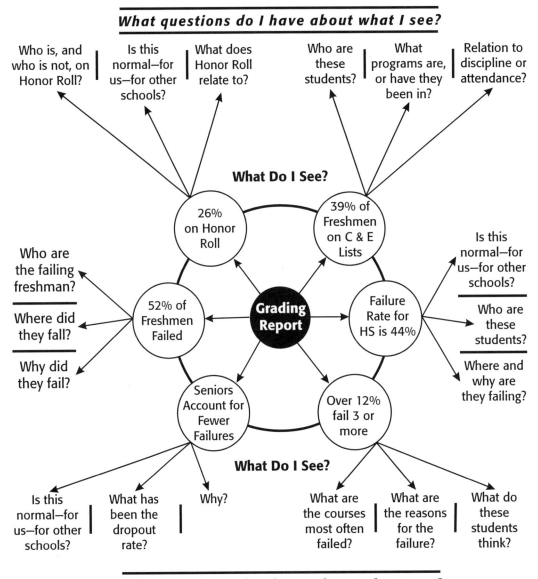

What questions do I have about what I see?

In the Questioning Data Process, the questions arrived at in step 12 provide direction for the next steps in seeking cause for student failures. Let's take a deeper look at the questions.

One easily notices that there is some repetition, with the same question being asked in response to several items that were seen. The questions can also be grouped into three categories: (a) those about the students, (b) those about the school, and (c) those about the school in comparison to itself over time and to other schools.

Questions About the Students

♦ Who are the failing freshmen?

♦ What do the students think about why they failed?

♦ Who is, and who is not, on honor roll?

Questions About the School and Its Processes

♦ Where did they fail?

♦ Why did they fail?

♦ What has been the dropout rate?

♦ Why do seniors account for fewer failures?

♦ What is the relationship to discipline and attendance?

♦ What support programs are, or have they been in?

♦ Who is, and who is not, on honor roll

♦ What other factors does honor roll relate to?

Questions About the School in Comparison to Itself Over Time and to Other Schools

♦ Is this normal for us? for other schools?

♦ What has been the dropout rate?

Some of these questions can be easily answered with data from other data sets. The problem in many schools, however, is that data has been so infrequently used that the data sets may be hard to locate or is simply "lost." Another problem encountered is that data sets are typically "owned" by different segments of the school system and are compiled using different formats and technologies. As schools move toward using data and developing data warehousing and mining, these problems will diminish over time. The hope is that schools will come to "know" at least as much about the learning progress of each and every of its students as the modern supermarket knows about a can of beans on its shelf.

Let's examine several of these questions further, starting with those focusing on the students.

The first question, "Who are the failing freshmen?" is a demographic question.

Much of this data is on hand, but other responses to this question may have to be researched more deeply. Disaggregation of data might include:

- Differences in gender

- Differences in socioeconomic level

- Differences in ethnicity

- Differences in primary language spoken at home

- Differences between children with identified disabilities and those with none.

- Differences in age and number of retentions

- Differences in student history such as sending school, teachers, etc.

- Differences in number of years student has been in this school

- Differences among "town" and "country" students—location of home

Depending upon the context of the analysis being made, there may be other issues that need to be explored. The disaggregation should include not only a description of the failing group (by gender, for example) but a comparison of the composition of the failing group to the passing group and to the total school population. An essential part of all root cause exercises is the "discovery" of new knowledge about the system, and, in this case, about its students. Out of this discovery comes new insight into possible areas of causation.

The second question, "What do the students think about why they failed?" is a perception question. It is doubtful that there is any data on this and, thus, to obtain the data, a survey needs to be developed and administered in a manner that will ensure a degree of both validity and reliability. In one school, guidance counselors were required to meet immediately with every one of their assigned students who had failed a course. It would be appropriate for a minimal one- or two-question survey to be taken during that meeting, recorded, computed, and analyzed in order to gain a better picture of the students' own perceptions regarding their failure. It would be equally easy to ask faculty, parents of failing students, and even students who pass, the same question to obtain perceptions from multiple groups. But this really goes beyond the scope of the question as phrased.

The third question, "Who is, and who is not, on honor roll?" is also a demographic question and can be answered in a similar manner to the first question.

The second set of questions deal with factors related to the school and its processes.

The first question, "Where did they fail?" is a demographic school issue. Because we are dealing with the June Grade Report, we need not ask about the "time" of failure because we know it is the final grade. In other contexts, it would be important to note the sequence of grades over the course of the year.

Teacher-given grades are a rich source of information about the student, teacher, and system. In this instance, however, we need to ask:

- In what department did the failures occur?

- In what subjects did the failures occur?

- In what classes did the failures occur?

- With what teachers did the failures occur?

The last two questions raise sensitive issues because they place a good deal of focus on individual members of the staff. If root cause analysis is conducted as a witch hunt, or to assign blame and retribution, it should not be started, or cooperated with, in the first place. Root cause analysis must be conducted within the context of systems thinking and trust, and with an understanding that 90 percent or more of the problems are caused by the system rather than the individual. Even if an individual teacher, or group of teachers, is identified as contributing to the "cause" of student failure, the questions remain: who recruited that teacher, who hired that teacher, who mentored, oriented, and tenured that teacher, who supported and developed that teacher, and what processes within the system allowed that teacher, or group of teachers, to become a block to student success rather than an enabler? It seems that we have passed the point of no return in our professional trek toward ever greater and more public accountability for what we do, and for what we do not do. Not to seek the answers to the issues listed above can easily be construed as dereliction of duty to our students. To use the answers to these questions alone, and not to connect them to other answers to other questions is equally wrong. An individual teacher, program, or building may have a very high percentage of failure while at the same time providing a high degree of value added to students who were placed because of their high beginning deficits.

The compilation of data showing the departments in which student failure occurred is contained in Figure 3.3.

Figure 3.3. Data Correlating Student Failures with Departments

Department	Enrollment	Number of Failures	Failures as Percent of Enrolled	Enrollment as Percent of School	Failures as Percent of School
English	834	142	17.0%	19.0%	19.5%
Social Studies	671	155	23.1%	15.3%	21.3%
Mathematics	594	93	15.7%	13.6%	12.8%
Science	586	155	26.5%	13.4%	21.3%
Foreign Language	391	26	6.6%	8.9%	3.6%
Business	432	57	13.2%	9.9%	7.8%
Art	284	41	14.4%	6.5%	5.6%
Music	198	0	0.0%	4.5%	0.0%
Technology Education	83	30	36.1%	1.9%	4.1%
Home and Careers	29	1	3.4%	.7%	.1%
Health	95	16	16.8%	2.2%	2.2%
Computer Program	100	4	4.0%	2.3%	0.6%
Vocational Education	81	7	8.6%	1.9%	1.0%
Total	4378	727	16.6%		

The same two-question process is applied to this new data set as were used originally:

Question 1: "What do we see in this data?"

Question 2: "What questions do we have about what we see?"

Although many issues are "seen" in this data set, the following items stand out in our search for the cause for student failure:

♦ 47% of all failure occurs in three departments (Social Studies, Science, and Technology Education), a total of 340 student failures.

♦ These three departments enroll only 31% of the students.

♦ Technology Education fails over a third of its students and produces failures at twice the percentage of its enrollment on a school-wide basis.

Although failures are distributed widely among the various departments, it appears that we have found three "hot spots" where failure is out of proportion to both enrollment and the department's "fair share."

What questions do we have about what we are seeing? Valid questions would include issues such as:

- Why do we have what appears to be excessive failure in these three departments?

- Where in these departments can we find the failure? Is it distributed across all courses or can it be localized to specific courses and teachers or groupings of students?

- What are the reasons for failure?

The ultimate question is: What can we do to prevent this high degree of failure? Once we know where and why students fail it becomes an easier task to seek solutions that will assist in preventing failure.

In digging into the third level of this discovery process, data was collected on where the failures were occurring, and it was disaggregated by grade level. Three segments of this data set are shown in Figure 3.4—the data for Social Studies, Science, and English for the freshman year. The data for English are used here as a comparison because that department's distribution of grades and failures approximates that of the school as a whole.

Figure 3.4. Third-Level Questioning Data

Course	Percent of Failing Averages			Enrollment	Mean Grade
	E/A	College	Local		
Social Studies 9			29.7%	74	65.6
Social Studies 9R		30.5%		108	73.6
Social Studies 9E	0.0%			25	89.7
General Science			34.3%	149	67.0
Earth Science		10.1%		79	76.0
English 9			23.5%	68	68.7
English 9R		8.9%		134	76.8
English 9A	0.0%			20	89.8

Key: R = College Prep, E = Enriched, A = Accelerated

What do we see in this data set? We see the following issues:

- Nearly 30 percent of local diploma students fail their course. (When this data was disaggregated by gender, failures were found among males in overwhelming numbers.)

- A substantially smaller number of college prep students fail

- No student in enriched or accelerated courses fails

- Over three times as many college prep social studies students failed as compared to college prep English students. This is the same cohort, although it appears that the English enrollment is even more diverse as a result of its larger size.

- When we look at the mean grade, we see that the means ascend as one moves from local, to college prep, to enriched or accelerated. Although on the surface this might seem logical, it also means that students in the local track find it nearly impossible to receive a score above 80 percent. If these courses were truly designed for the population they serve, should it not be possible for larger numbers of students to achieve?—just a thought.

By disaggregating school process data by student tracking and gender data we have crossed over into the sphere of questions regarding the students. Because of what was being seen, data was also accumulated for several previous years, and this showed that the patterns found in this June report were relatively stable from year to year. This June's report was not an aberration. What we were discovering was a pattern, a culture, that seemed to sustain high rates of failure, particularly among male, local diploma students. The answer to the question: "Is this normal for us?" was a resounding yes.

In order to answer the question: "Is this normal for other schools?" the principal had to call upon his collegial relationships with other principals. In this case, he sought help from five similar schools in the same athletic league, and asked them for data similar to that contained on the June grading report. Part of this data is shown in Figure 3.5.

Figure 3.5. Comparative Data from Other Schools

	Genny Eric HS	School A	School B	School C	School D	School E
Enrollment	802	346	551	325	125	868
Percent of honor roll	26%	36%	21%	21%	13%	27%
Percent with GPA 65–69	13%	8%	7%	12%	3%	4%
Percent with GPA 0–64	14%	1%	7%	13%	0%	3%
Percent with F	44%	18%	33%	33%	24%	17%
F/Student	.91	.33	.71	.56	.63	.30
State testing: percent of grade cohort that passed the exam						
Social Studies 11	51%	63%	38%	67%	32%	70%
Earth Science 9	35%	44%	38%	39%	38%	52%
English 11	53%	70%	46%	48%	44%	79%

In answer to the question: "Is this normal for other schools?," the resounding answer is NO! Only School C came close to the 27% of students with a final grade point average (GPA) below 70. The other four schools all had significantly lower percentages. Likewise, no other school had as high a percentage of students with at least one F.

When initially challenged with this data, the Genny Eric High School staff claimed it was their high standards that caused the high failure rate. But a look at the state testing data from the six schools indicates that the "high standards" did not convert to high achievement on state tests as compared to the other schools.

In social studies, three other schools enabled a higher percentage of the tested cohort to succeed; in earth science, five other schools achieved a higher percentage; and, in English, two other schools achieved at higher levels.

Although a lot can be "seen" in this data set and its extensions, an interesting discovery is the data submitted by School E. This school is slightly larger than the Genny Eric High School, has a similar percentage on honor roll, but has far fewer students being graded with a GPA below 70. In addition, only 17 percent of its students go home with an F in June, and the ratio of F's to students is a third that of the Genny Eric High School. Yet, on the state exams School E consistently outscores not only the Genny Eric High School, but the other four schools as well.

To be fair, other data sets indicate that School E has higher household income and fewer students in poverty, but the school spends about the same dollars per student and its student/teacher ratio is higher. In an environment where all students are expected to achieve at least proficiently, income and poverty rates may be informative, but they can no longer serve as justification for failure. The major question remains: what is School E doing to achieve low student failure and high student success on state testing. It would seem that this initial benchmarking of data should lead to a benchmarking on-site visit to School E. (Benchmarking will be discussed in greater detail in Chapter 7.)

As the other questions about the first data set are researched and answered, the pieces of the root cause puzzle begin to come together. As can be seen, other questions and leads develop that must also be explored. Eventually, one "sees" that the solution to the issue of high failure is more complex than simply changing a textbook, or introducing a new program. It is evident in this example of the Genny Eric High School Grading Report that we are dealing with a far more complex issue of school culture and beliefs that need to be modified in order to enable greater success in the classroom and on state testing.

Obviously, this depth of Questioning Data cannot be accomplished over a one day staff development session—but it can be started. It takes leadership and commitment for the process to continue and for the grunt work of data gathering to be accomplished. After each session, the team should confirm assignments and expect that the homework will be accomplished by its next meeting—generally no sooner than two weeks nor longer than four weeks away. An interval of less than two weeks does not provide sufficient time for locating or preparing data in response to the questions. Intervals longer than four weeks risk having the process become stagnant, and much time is taken to "recap" what has been forgotten.

Example 2: Using the Questioning Data Process to Assess a System

The Hilltop Central School District decided to investigate the permanent record cards of all graduating seniors to examine various aspects of their system as well as to "see" what students had accomplished in order to earn a diploma. A partial presentation of three years of data examined is shown in Figure 3.6.

Figure 3.6. The Hilltop Central School District: Partial Summary of Graduate Permanent Record Cards

	Class of 1999			Class of 2000			Class of 2001			3 Year Total		
	Total	F	M	Total	F	M	Total	F	M	Total	F	M
Number of Graduates	56	29	26	46	23	23	48	30	18	149	82	67
Number of A Diplomas[1]	30	21	9	21	13	8	25	18	7	76	52	24
Percent of A Diplomas[1]	55%	72%	35%	46%	57%	35%	52%	60%	39%	51%	63%	36%
Number of IEP Diplomas[2]	4	0	4	1	1	0	0	0	0	5	1	4
Number of HS F's	81	25	56	39	8	31	45	16	29	165	49	116
Percent of HS F's		31%	69%		21%	79%		36%	64%		30%	70%
Number of Grads with F	26	10	16	16	4	12	17	7	10	59	21	38
Percent of Grads with F		38%	62%		25%	75%		41%	59%		36%	64%
Number of Vocational Students	9	1	8	5	2	3	9	4	5	23	7	16
Percent of Vocational Students	16%	3%	31%	11%	9%	13%	19%	13%	28%	15%	9%	24%

	Class of 1999			Class of 2000			Class of 2001			3 Year Total		
	Total	F	M	Total	F	M	Total	F	M	Total	F	M
Average Class Rank	24	19.7	31.2	22.7	16.5	28.7	23.4	18	32.2			
Number in Top Half	25	18	7	21	13	8	25	20	5	71	51	20
Percent in Top Half	45%	62%	27%	46%	57%	35%	52%	67%	28%	48%	63%	30%
Number of Unranked	6	1	5	3	1	2	5	3	2	17	5	12
Average Number of Units	24.8	26.4	23.1	23.9	24.5	24.3	24.9	25.2	24.5	24.6	25.4	23.9
Number Below 22 Units	8	0	8	4	2	2	5	3	2	17	5	12
Number Taking SAT	31	22	9	27	15	12	28	21	7	86	58	28
Percent Taking SAT	56%	76%	35%	59%	65%	52%	58%	70%	39%	58%	71%	42%
Average SAT V	503	508	491	501	538	454	478	479	474	494	505	471
Average SAT M	515	514	518	526	540	508	481	481	481	507	509	504

[1] *Academic Diploma*
[2] *Diplomas for Students with Disabilities*

What did they "see" in the data that was felt to be important and what questions did they have about what they saw?

- ♦ Differences between female and male success and achievement.
  - • Is this normal for us and for other schools?
  - • What are the perceptions for "Why?"
  - • How do people feel about this data?
  - • Are there groupings to explore other than gender?
- ♦ Males have more "F's" than females

- Where are the "F's"?

- Why are the "F's"?

- Were there any remedial actions before failure?

- What is the distribution of grades by year and by subject?

♦ Males have fewer academic diplomas

- What requirements for an academic diploma are missing?

- Is this a student decision or is it a result of failure?

- Are there linkages with post-graduation plans?

This information is shown in Figure 3.7.

Overall, there was a pattern of superior female achievement and recognition in this school that seemed to be sustained over a long period of time and that appeared to be ingrained in its culture and perhaps the culture of its community as well.

In order to meet state regulations requiring that all students meet requirements for an academic diploma and successfully achieve a minimum of 22 units of credit, the school has to deal with this cultural issue, which seems to be centered around different expectations for the genders.

Again, as in the preceding example regarding the Genny Eric High School, what the team sees in the data, and the questions that its members have about what they see lead them to study ever deeper sets of data that provide greater insight into their system, its results, and its needs. This is a process of discovery that leads to root causes.

Figure 3.7. Questioning Data Schematic

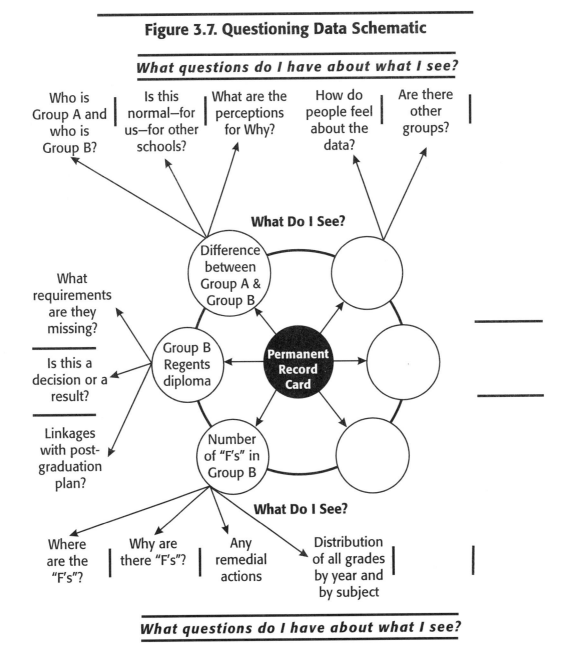

What questions do I have about what I see?

Who is Group A and who is Group B?

Is this normal—for us—for other schools?

What are the perceptions for Why?

How do people feel about the data?

Are there other groups?

What Do I See?

Difference between Group A & Group B

What requirements are they missing?

Is this a decision or a result?

Linkages with post-graduation plan?

Group B Regents diploma

Permanent Record Card

Number of "F's" in Group B

What Do I See?

Where are the "F's"?

Why are there "F's"?

Any remedial actions

Distribution of all grades by year and by subject

What questions do I have about what I see?

The Diagnostic Tree Process

The Diagnostic Tree Process is a tool that can be used following the identification of a specific Level One red-flag issue. A "red flag" is an obvious discrepancy between expectation and result. Similar processes have been developed and are being used in different contexts. All of these processes, however, have as their goal the identification and elimination of causal factors for problem issues.

The Diagnostic Tree provides a structured discovery process that focuses on the whole of the school system, moving from the particular issue to ever broader levels until causal issues are found and proven. It should be cautioned, however, not to allow the structured nature of the process to restrict creative thinking regarding causation. In the hands of some, the Diagnostic Tree can become a type of checklist of all known causes, thereby eliminating from discussion all unknown causes. This must be guarded against.

Figure 3.8 shows a basic Diagnostic Tree through three levels: (a) the "Red Flag" Identification Level, (b) Location Level, and the (c) Sequence 1 Hypotheses Level. A Diagnostic Tree Template can be found at the back of this chapter in Figure 3.23.

Figure 3.8. Basic Diagnostic Tree—Math 8 Achievement

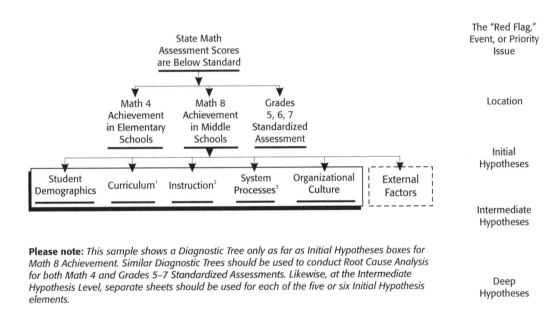

Please note: *This sample shows a Diagnostic Tree only as far as Initial Hypotheses boxes for Math 8 Achievement. Similar Diagnostic Trees should be used to conduct Root Cause Analysis for both Math 4 and Grades 5–7 Standardized Assessments. Likewise, at the Intermediate Hypothesis Level, separate sheets should be used for each of the five or six Initial Hypothesis elements.*

The first level is the "red-flag" event or priority issue that is under analysis. It is usually identified as the result of examination of a Level One data set on key indicators of student success. In this example the issue is student achievement in the area of math as measured by state and other standardized assessments.

The second level identifies more specific "locations" of the problem issue. In this example, the locations have been identified as elementary achievement on math grade 4 and middle school grade 8 state examinations, as well as on standardized testing in middle school grades 5, 6, and 7.

At the third level, very broad hypotheses areas are identified regarding possible location of the causes. Because the focus is on causes within schools, there are only five major hypothesis boxes. These contain issues related to: student demographics, curriculum, instruction, school system processes, and organizational culture. All potential elements of causation within the school can be assigned to one of these five areas. If a team decided to visit factors of external causation, a sixth box at this level would be added. There is typically more need for work within a school, however, without adding the responsibility for things over which it has little control. If a school sees the need for "remediating" external deficiencies and has the ability to do so, such remediation should definitely become part of the school improvement process, and, therefore, it would become the sixth branch on the tree.

The hypotheses involving student demographics may identify traditional issues such as gender, ethnicity, language spoken, disabilities, and age, but can also cover other issues such as student academic history, previous courses and teachers, longevity in the system, attendance, disciplinary records, location within the school district, degree of engagement and participation, and any other factors that the team thinks may be causing the "red-flag" issue to come about.

In one school, it was felt that a much higher percentage of failing students resulted because those students were actually transfers from other districts. This "opinion" can easily be proven by looking at demographic data for failing students and disaggregating it by the number of years within the district. In this case, although there were transfers into the system, they did not prove to be instrumental in adding to the number of students failing standardized assessments.

In another district, poor attendance was thought to be an underlying cause for weak student performance in the English. Upon examination, however, it was found that there was no relationship between student attendance and achievement, and, if really pushed, it appeared that students who were absent more frequently achieved more. A new attendance policy would become an unnecessary patch on the system.

A third district found a very strong relationship between student achievement, participation in extracurricular activities, and gender. Generally, girls achieved more than boys and comprised two-thirds of all students engaged in extracurricular activities. As participation increased, so did achievement. The original concept was to study student "engagement" in school as measured by the students' participation in activities outside of required classes, with engagement being seen as essential for high levels of achievement. Data was collected for all students in grades 7–12 for a period of three years, and patterns emerged that indicated that students became involved in activities in seventh or eighth grade and generally maintained their involvement. Students not involved early in their school career remained uninvolved throughout their years in school. The district then went on to examine issues they felt might be inhibiting participation within their unique district context. Ultimately, the district discovered that many students were not aware of the full program of activities offered, were not overly encouraged to participate, and that some students had interest in activities not offered by the school.

The curriculum hypothesis box contains just two issues—curriculum alignment and balance. Alignment of curriculum with state standards and assessments is necessary to permit high levels of student achievement. The content that is tested must be taught. At the same time, what is taught must be in balance with state expectations. A curriculum might be aligned with state standards but be out of balance in terms of the time and detail devoted to each element. The struggle for alignment and balance is greatly aided by various types of curriculum mapping and staff development efforts that focus on that purpose.

The instruction hypothesis box can contain many potential causal factors, among which are: instructional strategies that parallel state standards and methods of assessment, materials, time allocation, classroom setting, methods, student grouping, student/teacher relationships, and numerous other factors, all of which can be again subdivided into smaller elements.

The system processes box can again include many factors. Staffing, for example, is a process that not only covers the assignment and continuing development of staff, but also the recruiting, hiring, supervision, evaluation and tenuring of staff. Scheduling, grading, and, budgeting are all large school processes that may have an impact on learning. So may transportation systems, food services, and guidance services. Policies and procedures for promotion and retention, for providing additional academic support, and for following up on absences may also be crucial leverage points for improving achievement of the key indicators of student success.

Organizational culture is a complex composite of history, values, assumptions, norms, and attitudes. Culture drives not only the organization's behavior, but the behavior of those within it as well. Organizational artifacts, such as schedules, furniture, allocation of space, and publications all attest to the culture underlying their selection and use. C. Robert Nelms, developer of the Phoenix approach to root cause analysis, identifies the elements of attitude, assumptions, and beliefs as "latent" root causes because they often remain hidden from view but underlie the behaviors and actions that may be identified as "root causes." Nelms asks the next "Why?"—"Why did they do it?". The answer often can be found in these "latent" elements. Organizational culture is, perhaps, a slightly broader concept, but it is also often "latent" in its impact. The culture of school can easily be taken for granted by those within it, and, therefore, it remains unseen as a possible area of cause. Culture may also be the most tender of the five areas to expose because it deals with issues that participants hold dear. Nevertheless, it must be considered in all root cause searches because it can drive, directly or indirectly, the other four critical areas.

Obviously, not all issues in all of these boxes can be investigated for every red-flag issue, at least not with the current state of data warehousing and mining. The facilitator's guidelines below are provided to assist the process of identifying the few high-potential hypotheses from the many with lesser potential.

Facilitator Guidelines

1. Explain the concept behind the logic tree while presenting the first three levels of the tree: Red Flag/Priority Issue, Location, and Initial Hypothesis elements.

2. If the group is larger than six, divide the group into subgroups no larger than six.

3. Ask each person to reflect on the Red Flag, Locations, and Initial Hypothesis elements to identify possible important causative factors under each of the four, or five, initial hypotheses.

An alternative would be to ask each of five small groups to focus on a single element. This will simplify the process, but will also exclude four-fifths of the participants from considering each of the elements. This can be somewhat corrected in step 6 when the whole group is asked to identify anything that is missing.

4. Individuals share in their small groups, and each small group is responsible for identifying and reporting out what they agree are possible important causative factors for each of the four elements.

5. Each small group reports out its items, giving one item for each of the five hypothesis elements. This continues until all items are reported for all elements. Items that are reported by more than one small group are noted, but are integrated or discarded.

6. The whole group is asked if there are any potential items that are missing. At this point, the facilitator may want to challenge the group if there are any obvious absences in what the group has identified. While remembering that the group still owns the content of this process, the facilitator should ensure that the process is honest and complete.

7. If the number of items under each hypothesis element is manageable—four to six—keep and explore them all. If there is a larger listing—seven or more—use a paretoing process to identify those that the group thinks are most important and likely possible causes.

8. Discuss how each item should be investigated, what data is needed, and how it will be developed and used to see its relation to the cause of the red-flag issue.

9. Identify responsibility for accomplishing the investigation and a timeline for its completion and reporting back to the whole team. Normally, a specific due date should be specified within four weeks.

11. Again, the verification process should be employed to share the work, thinking, and product of the team with all stakeholder groups. Although the team should not wait for the completion of the verification process to begin its deeper investigation, it is important to share the work, receive feedback, and integrate feedback appropriately as the process moves forward. The updated schematic with a brief narrative can be used as the means of communication.

As the work using the Diagnostic Tree progresses, keep the schematic up-to-date. The intent is to either prove beyond a doubt that an item is indeed related and is a possible cause, or that it is not related and, therefore, cannot be a possible cause.

As helpful as any of these processes are, the reflection, discussion, dialogue, and thinking generated by their use is vastly more important. If used consistently in problem solving throughout the district, the Diagnostic Tree approach will encourage changes in how people see problems and their causes, and in the selection of strategies of improvement.

Figure 3.9 shows what a single district identified as potential causative issues (Intermediate Hypotheses) for each of five major initial elements. All have been placed on a single sheet along with additional information to help explain the contents. This single sheet can be used as a communications tool with various stakeholder groups and for purposes of verification of the content.

Figure 3.9. Extended Diagnostic Tree—Math 8 Achievement

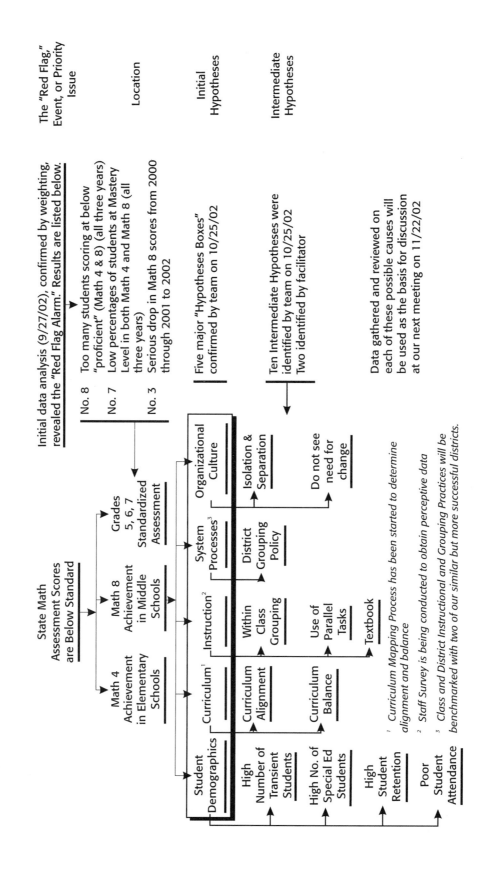

The column of information to the right of the Diagnostic Tree helps to explain the progression of the process and identifies the dates when each element was confirmed or arrived at. Note that the establishment of the three "locations of concern" is supported by reference to specific data sets which back up the selection of these locations. The use of five boxes, excluding the "external issues," box was confirmed by the team on 10/25/02. At that same meeting, the team completed its process of identifying potential causes for the poor student achievement.

Under Student Demographics, the team identified four intermediate hypotheses: the high number of transient students, the high number of special education students, a high student retention rate, and poor student attendance. Each of these issues will be researched and reported upon at the next meeting of the team.

1. Investigation of transient students will use test score data combined with the number of years that a student has been within the school system to determine if there is a relationship between time in district and the score.

2. The impact of the number of special education students will be examined in at least two ways. Is the number of special education students higher than in similar districts? And, is there a relationship between being identified as having special needs and the assessment score?

3. Students who have been retained, once, twice, and three times or more will be identified and the relationship to assessment scores examined.

4. Student attendance in school will be examined in relation to assessment scores. Another, although more complex comparison, would be to obtain actual student attendance in the math classes as compared to their scores, because students may often be marked present in school but "miss" math class for one reason or another.

Responsibility for completing each of these tasks prior to the next meeting needs to be assumed by a team member, although other human resources may actually be engaged in completing each analysis. If at all possible, the results of each of these analysis should be shared with the team prior to the meeting to make the best use of meeting time.

It was found that the district indeed had nearly twice as many students with special instructional needs as the average and that these students did not do well on the state assessments. Student attendance, retention, and movement into the district did not appear as factors. This will lead to another series of "deep hypotheses" regarding why the district had such a high number of students with special needs and how instruction can be improved to enable them to achieve minimum state standards.

Both items under Curriculum—Curriculum Alignment and Curriculum Balance—were already under investigation through a consultant lead curriculum mapping process. The results of this process will be used to further align the school's curriculum with the standards of the state.

Preliminary information from the curriculum mapping process indicated that there were indeed large gaps in the content being taught when compared to state standards and that there were also issues of imbalance and timing—some items not being taught until after the assessment. These needed to be remedied through changes in the curriculum and through staff development.

Three items were identified under Instruction: (a) Within Class Grouping, (b) the Use of Parallel Tasks, and (c) the Textbook. It was felt that information about the first two items could best be obtained through a survey of K–8 faculty, and the third through benchmarking with previously identified similar school districts in the region. A brief survey was developed and administered, and the results were tabulated and distributed prior to the team's next meeting. It provided important insight into math instructional practices across nine grade levels. An interesting outcome of the textbook benchmarking was the discovery that one of the high achieving schools used the same textbook—they just used it in a different way.

The single item of grouping, or the lack of tracking, students was identified as a possible system issue. The team decided to find out how the two benchmarking schools with much higher math achievement went about differentiating their instruction. Research into "best practice" might also be advisable in studying this issue.

The process facilitator identified several cultural strands that became evident through the work and discussion of the team. The belief that the school was accomplishing all that it could given the students at hand was being challenged by new leadership and the beliefs of what had been a minority of the staff. A history of isolation and separation was again being challenged by efforts to bring K–12 staff together to view problems within a systems context.

The purpose here is not to chronicle in complete detail the continuing use of the Diagnostic Tree within the context of a single district's school improvement process, but rather to illustrate enough segments of its use to provide both understanding and knowledge of its potential as a tool for seeking root causes. Let's, however, take the process just one step further as presented on a series of schematics in Figures 3.10–3.14.

Figure 3.10. Detailed Diagnostic Tree—Math 8 Achievement: Variation 1

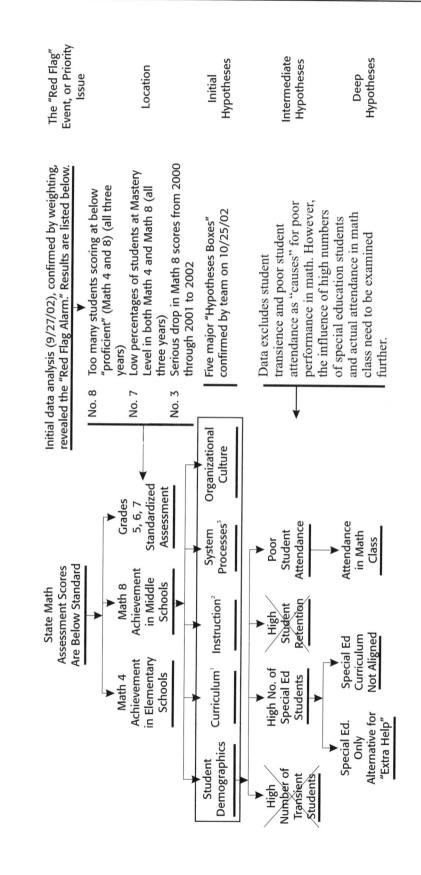

Figure 3.11. Detailed Diagnostic Tree—Math 8 Achievement: Variation 2

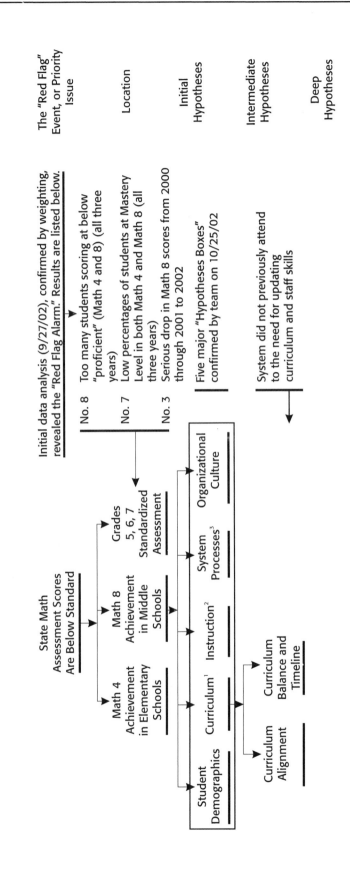

Initial data analysis (9/27/02), confirmed by weighting, revealed the "Red Flag Alarm." Results are listed below.

No. 8   Too many students scoring at below "proficient" (Math 4 and 8) (all three years)

No. 7   Low percentages of students at Mastery Level in both Math 4 and Math 8 (all three years)

No. 3   Serious drop in Math 8 scores from 2000 through 2001 to 2002

Five major "Hypotheses Boxes" confirmed by team on 10/25/02

System did not previously attend to the need for updating curriculum and staff skills

The "Red Flag" Event, or Priority Issue

Location

Initial Hypotheses

Intermediate Hypotheses

Deep Hypotheses

State Math Assessment Scores Are Below Standard

Math 4 Achievement in Elementary Schools

Math 8 Achievement in Middle Schools

Grades 5, 6, 7 Standardized Assessment

Student Demographics

Curriculum[1]   Instruction[2]   System Processes[3]   Organizational Culture

Curriculum Alignment

Curriculum Balance and Timeline

Figure 3.12. Detailed Diagnostic Tree—Math 8 Achievement: Variation 3

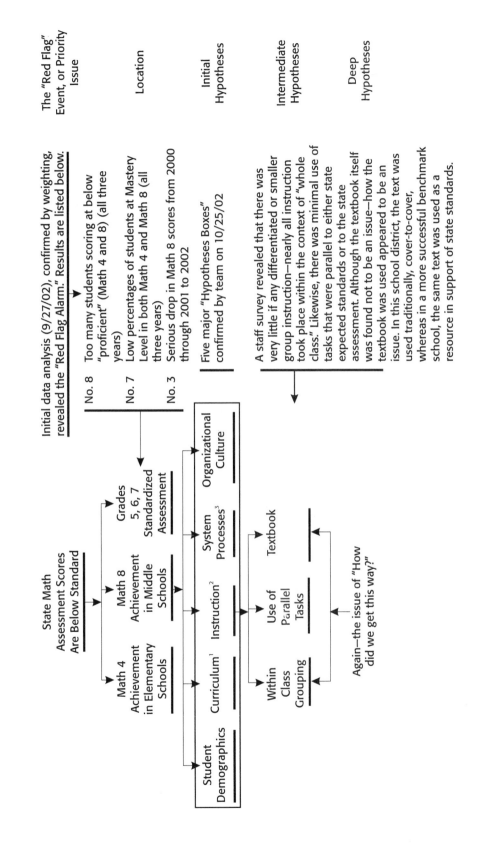

Figure 3.13. Detailed Diagnostic Tree—Math 8 Achievement: Variation 4

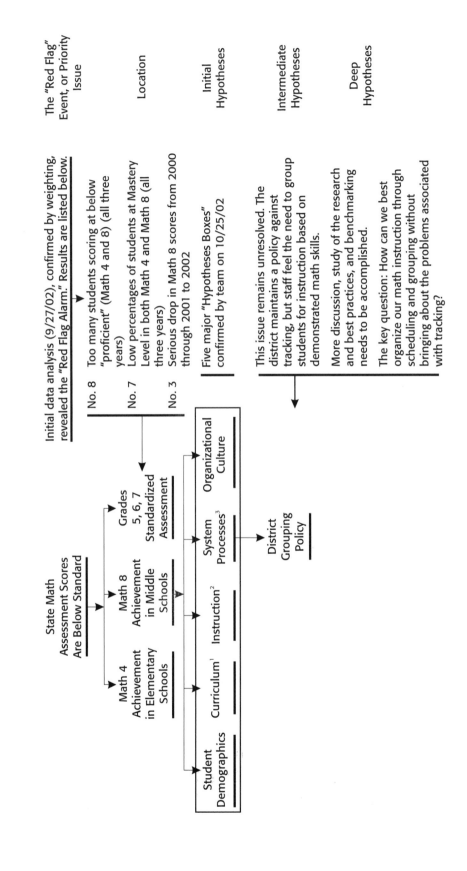

The "Red Flag" Event, or Priority Issue

Location

Initial Hypotheses

Intermediate Hypotheses

Deep Hypotheses

Initial data analysis (9/27/02), confirmed by weighting, revealed the "Red Flag Alarm." Results are listed below.

No. 8 — Too many students scoring at below "proficient" (Math 4 and 8) (all three years)

No. 7 — Low percentages of students at Mastery Level in both Math 4 and Math 8 (all three years)

No. 3 — Serious drop in Math 8 scores from 2000 through 2002

Five major "Hypotheses Boxes" confirmed by team on 10/25/02

This issue remains unresolved. The district maintains a policy against tracking, but staff feel the need to group students for instruction based on demonstrated math skills.

More discussion, study of the research and best practices, and benchmarking needs to be accomplished.

The key question: How can we best organize our math instruction through scheduling and grouping without bringing about the problems associated with tracking?

State Math Assessment Scores Are Below Standard

Math 4 Achievement in Elementary Schools

Math 8 Achievement in Middle Schools

Grades 5, 6, 7 Standardized Assessment

Student Demographics

Curriculum[1]

Instruction[2]

System Processes[3]

Organizational Culture

District Grouping Policy

Figure 3.14. Detailed Diagnostic Tree—Math 8 Achievement: Variation 5

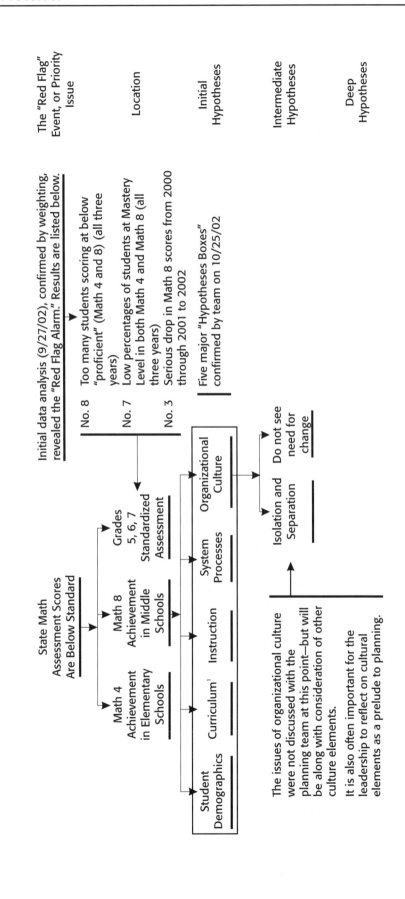

In Figure 3.10, the focus is on the element of student demographics. Two of the items have been proven null: the high number of transient students and the student retention rate. One item, the high number of students in special education, has proven to be related to poor performance on the assessment. Deeper hypotheses suggest that the special education math curriculum may not be aligned with state standards and that the high number of special education students is more a reflection of the lack of other sources of student support than it is a reflection of the actual number of handicapped students within the district. Although poor student attendance in school was found to be null, the issue regarding actual attendance in math class was raised and needs to be explored further. If indeed poorly performing students are missing more math classes than better performing students, the district then needs to find out why. Is it the result of pull-out programs, student cutting, extracurricular activities, etc.? Once it is proven that attendance in math class is a related factor, and causes for the absences are found, steps can be taken to reduce the degree of absences.

Likewise, in studying the relationship of special education students to poor math performance, the district needs to further study the alignment of special education curriculum to the standards, the diversity of handicapping conditions among students, and what are the causes for such a high density of identified students. Further knowledge of the total picture will lead to a better understanding of how to approach this issue with wisdom.

Figure 3.11 focuses on the element of curriculum. The curriculum mapping process revealed lack of alignment with state standards for math as well as an imbalance in the weighting of certain content segments. In addition, there was an issue of timing where certain required content was not taught until after the state assessment. Each of these issues, now having been identified, will provide the focus for continued curriculum and staff development.

One could stop at this intermediate level and work to improve student math achievement, but an important question remains: Why did the system not attend to these issues previously? Are there basic elements or processes within the system that cause delayed response to such critical issues? Are there cultural reasons as well? If so, they are no doubt manifested in areas other than math achievement as well. In order to improve the system, and to reduce the frequency of future iterations of this type of deficiency, the underlying system causes should be sought and dissolved. Deep hypotheses regarding this failure might include: the lack of leadership, an ingrained culture of stagnation, lack of resources, low expectations for system, self, and students, and system disconnectedness. Again, to truly improve the system's ability to meet the needs of students, these deeper issues must be sought and resolved.

Figure 3.12 focuses on the element of instruction, specifically the issues of within-class grouping, use of parallel tasks, and the textbook used. To gain better insight into these issues, a brief staff survey was developed and issued.

The responses revealed that there was very little, if any, differentiated or smaller group instruction—nearly all instruction took place within the context of the "whole class." Likewise, there was minimal use of tasks that were parallel to either state-expected standards or to the state assessment. Interestingly, though a high-performing benchmark school used the same textbook, they used it in a completely different way—as a resource in support of their state standard-driven curriculum, rather than as a "cover-to-cover" defacto curriculum.

The response to these findings can be found in continuing staff development focused on the creation and use of parallel tasks, greater differentiation of instruction and linkage to the work being done to align and balance the curriculum with state standards. Finally, there are also the issues of "How did we get this way?" and "What can we do to dissolve these deeper system causes?"

Figure 3.13 focuses on the single-system process that came under scrutiny, the grouping policy. Although still unresolved in this example, the issue requires further study of the research and best practice in this area, as well as benchmarking with higher-achieving districts. The key is in finding ways to better differentiate instruction while avoiding the negative aspects of static grouping of students.

Figure 3.14 deals with the issue of *Organizational Culture* and two elements that were identified by the facilitator as the result of observing team member statements and learning more about the district history. Although this is superficial at best, the discussion regarding these two elements within the whole context of culture may very well lead to the identification of other cultural elements that underlie district and individual actions and behaviors.

It is more than likely that not all roots of the "red-flag" issue have been laid bare during this first attempt at using the Diagnostic Tree process. It should be evident, however, that the process has stimulated much deeper inquiry, discussion, and reflection, and, as a result, it has indeed helped to identify specific causal issues and the strategies necessary to dissolve them. The process has also enabled much deeper knowledge of the system, a prelude to more effective decision making in the future.

Once again, the long-term intent is not only to develop skills in the use of specific root cause analysis tools, but to incorporate them in the daily routines of the school in such a way that the fundamental way that the school goes about its decision making is changed to include the pause for deep reflection on cause.

In the beginning of this section on the Diagnostic Tree, caution was urged regarding the potential for it to become a type of static checklist seen as containing all possible root cause factors. In spite of this fear, the partial listing below is provided as an incomplete illustrative stimulus for understanding the variety and scope of each of the five major hypothesis areas. Many of the elements identified can be broken down further into numerous subelements.

- ◆ Student Demographics
  - Gender
  - Student socioeconomic status
  - Ethnicity/race
  - Handicapping condition
  - Language spoken at home
  - Student's primary language
  - Years in this school district
  - Membership in school programs such as remediation
  - Age
  - Retention record
  - Academic average
  - Rank in class or academic average
  - Assessment scores
  - Participation rates
  - Attendance rates
  - Disciplinary incidents
  - School groupings
- ◆ Curriculum
  - Alignment with state standards
  - Balance with state standards
  - Timeline of presentations
  - Time on task
  - Staff knowledge regarding curriculum
- ◆ Instruction
  - Methods
  - Materials
  - Setting
  - Time on task
  - Expectations
  - Student engagement with content/process

- Student motivation
- Student attainment of prerequisite skills
- Teacher training and skills (certification?)
- Teaching of curriculum
- Instructional tasks parallel to state assessments/standards

♦ School Processes

- Human resources—staffing, recruiting, tenuring
- Supervision and evaluation—aligned with school's purpose and goals
- Staff development
- Financial—alignment of budget with school's purpose and goals
- Grading—student assessment/evaluation
- Scheduling and student programming
- Grouping
- Planning and continuous improvement
- Monitoring of student achievement
- Program evaluation
- Communication within and without
- Partnering
- Leadership
- Custodial services
- Transportation services
- Office support services

♦ Organizational Culture

- Values and beliefs
- Assumptions
- Philosophy
- Attitudes
- Norms
- Artifacts
- History

The Creative Root Cause Analysis Process

Not all educational root cause analysis has the luxury of having significant hard data upon which to build an investigation. In some instances, the data is in the form of observations, hunches, perceptions, and even feelings that do not lend themselves easily to typical numerical review. The *Creative Root Cause Analysis* process (CRCA) was developed by Dr. Jack L. Oxenrider, Executive Director of the Dow Leadership Center at Hillsdale College, Hillsdale, Michigan, as a means of incorporating "both the creative and the analytical into a powerful, dynamic way to solve complex problems at the root of origin." It has been used with great success, in a wide variety of settings, over a period of many years. Very thorough training programs are available through the Dow Leadership Center, as are materials and resources to successfully learn and facilitate the process (www.creativerootcauseanalysis.com). The following example of how the Creative Root Cause Analysis Process can be used is shared with permission from Dr. Oxenrider.

Five individuals, all involved with a piloted statewide comprehensive planning process, arrived at Hillsdale College for a two-day training session on Creative Root Cause Analysis. Although the immediate purpose was to learn the CRCA process, it soon became apparent that the learning could take place within the context of an important issue related to the comprehensive planning pilot. The "probing question" that this team of five agreed upon was:

> Why is there lack of statewide clarity on the concept and utilization of comprehensive planning as a tool to increase student achievement and district effectiveness?"

The evidence for this situation rested in the fact that each of the five team members had ample experience in seeing that districts, and even the State Education Department, did not understand, embrace, utilize, or adopt comprehensive planning to the extent deemed necessary to improve student achievement on a broad scale. Although there were some numbers that could be used, such as the number of districts piloting the comprehensive planning model, most of the "evidence" was anecdotal and experiential. There was consensus among the five participants, for example, that there was slight uniformity of understanding across the whole of the state regarding the foundations of comprehensive planning and key elements of the piloted model.

The Creative Root Cause Analysis training session provided a facilitated forum in which to learn the CRCA process and its underlying concepts. CRCA teaches a disciplined approach to both a team problem-solving process and a team communication cycle. These are used throughout the session to stimulate discussion, sharing of views, and arrival at consensus regarding the issues of cause and what to do about them.

Working both individually and as a team, the group of five initially identified 38 possible issues in answer to the probing question. These were discussed in detail and categorized into the following groupings:

- Logistics and infrastructure of the pilot.

- Culture of the schools.

- Understanding of the comprehensive planning model.

- The state education department

- Understanding of the concept of "systems."

The 38 potential issues, along with a number of additional issues that were identified in discussion, were all placed in one of these five categories. The issues were further refined, combined, and reduced in order to provide a clearer picture of what this group thought were major contributing causes to the probing question.

As this process of discovery continued, the following major roots underlying many of these issues were then identified, using both the team problem-solving process and the team communication cycle.

- Lack of clarity, simplicity, and uniformity in publications/materials.

- Inadequate infrastructure for dissemination of training.

- Lack of an effective means of communicating to all involved.

- Incomplete training for everyone, particularly planning facilitators.

Strategies identified to dissolve these roots were again developed using both the team problem-solving process and the team communication cycle. The team agreed to bring the following suggested strategies back to the whole of the comprehensive planning steering committee for consideration and implementation.

- Establishing a comprehensive planning facilitators academy that would "teach" a curriculum designed to provide uniform understanding and skills in support of the comprehensive planning pilot.

- Developing enhanced, but simplified, uniform support materials for facilitators, school districts, and those interested in learning more.

- Strengthening the infrastructure of the comprehensive planning team through more regular meetings, a listserv and Web site.

- Expanding membership in the steering committee to include greater diversity of representation.

◆ Seeking out a high-level leader within the state education department as a project "champion."

These items were reported back to the full steering committee at its next meeting, and, after discussion, steps were taken and responsibilities were assigned to implement each of the suggestions. The two days spent in training yielded rich results, not only in the skills acquired, but in the products that were of immediate use in strengthening the comprehensive planning pilot project.

This *Creative Root Cause Analysis* (CRCA) process did not rely on traditional numerical data in its approach to seeking root cause. It did, however, make extensive use of perceptive data presented by five individuals with in-depth knowledge and experience with this issue. In turn, the products from the CRCA session were returned to the steering committee (a larger group of equally experienced, but more diverse, indidivuals) for verification. The best *proof* of the effectiveness of the process is the improvement in clarity and increased utilization of comprehensive planning following the implementation of the five strategies.

The Five Whys

The process of the *Five Whys* goes back to the early days of the Total Quality Movement (TQM) in Japan and was used as a simple method for digging down through the layers of cause to the root cause. It is thought that after answering "Why" a minimum of five times, that one can find, or get much closer to the root cause. An example:

Team:	*Why* do we have so many class tardies?
Students:	Because we do not have enough time.
Team:	*Why* don't you have enough time to get from one class to another?
Students:	Because the passing time is only four minutes and we have to get from one end of the building to another and sometimes stop at our locker or go to the rest room.
Team:	*Why* is the passing time between classes only four minutes?
Principal:	Because we wanted to reduce the time that students were in the halls.
Team:	*Why* did we want to reduce the time that students were in the halls?
Principal:	Because we wanted to reduce disciplinary problems.
Team:	*Why* did we want to reduce disciplinary problems?
Principal:	We wanted to improve school safety and climate.

Not having enough time between classes was only the most immediate or proximate cause for students being tardy. Even reducing discipline problems in the hall was not the deepest root cause for tardiness. Rather, it was the desire to improve overall school safety and climate.

So often, however, we stop at the level of the symptom and never ask the first "Why"—marking a student tardy and perhaps assigning detention. Some may attempt to "patch" the symptom by adding a warning bell one minute before class, making punishment for tardiness more severe, or even instructing staff to stand at their classroom doors in order to wave the students in. These efforts do not deal with the fundamental problem: the need for more time between classes while maintaining safety and a positive climate.

The Five Why Process is a good model for the concept of root cause analysis, and the example above is a fine illustration of the law of unintended consequences. Although the Five Why process is a tool for simple problem solving and root identification, it is not often sufficiently robust to serve frequently as the means for discovering root causes within the complexity of most schools. It does serve, however, as a sound model for the necessity of digging deeply to find cause.

Some time ago, a school building lost its supply of fresh water as the result of a broken water main. School was closed a full day until the main could be repaired. It was obvious that the water main had been shattered, but the school did not ask the next why. It was assumed that the working of frost and a nearby stone had taken their toll. Within a year, the water main broke a second time, this time in a different place. Again the school shut down until repairs were made. The water main now had two "patches" on it. Still, no one delved into why the pipe had broken. It appeared to be just a coincidence caused by natural events. Then the pipe broke a third time, necessitating the closing of school yet again. This time, it was obvious that the breaking was more than coincidence and that something other than natural causes were at work. Ultimately it was discovered that the pipe was very brittle and that it could not withstand what it was called upon to do. The whole water main was replaced and the breakage stopped. Although the immediate problem was solved for the school, unanswered questions remained regarding "why" the pipe was brittle, and if it had to do with its manufacturing or with the contractor installing the wrong type of pipe to begin with. In order to prevent similar problems from emerging again, and perhaps to assign responsibility for the cost of repair, the additional "why's" should have been asked and their answers sought.

One can not help but reflect upon the strong parallelism between the Five Why's and an old 15th-century folk saying that George Herbert, Ben Franklin and others have so rightly passed on to us:

For want of a nail the shoe was lost.
For want of a shoe the horse was lost.
For want of a horse the rider was lost.
For want of a rider the battle was lost.
For want of a battle the kingdom was lost.
And all for the want of a horseshoe nail.

Indeed, the location of the root is sometimes very far from the ultimate effect and, as Ben Franklin noted in 1758, "A little neglect may breed great mischief."

Force Field Analysis

Kurt Lewin presented the concept of Force Field Analysis in 1951[1] and it has since been used extensively in a wide variety of settings and circumstances. In RCA, Force Field Analysis is both a useful tool for constructive brainstorming as well as a means of reporting out the work of the planning team.

Lewin conceived that all organizations, systems, processes, etc., are subject to opposing forces that, in stable contexts, are balanced. This balance causes the system to be held in a static position—unchanged. In order to move the organization, in order to change, it is necessary for the forces holding it in place to become unbalanced. Lewin identified these forces as driving forces and restraining forces. Driving forces apply pressure on the system to move in a direction of change, perhaps toward new goals. The restraining forces, on the other hand, apply pressure on the system to remain in place or even to return to older goals. Figure 3.15 below provides a simple model of how a force field analysis template can be drawn.

---

1 *Field theory in social science.* (1951). New York: Harper & Row

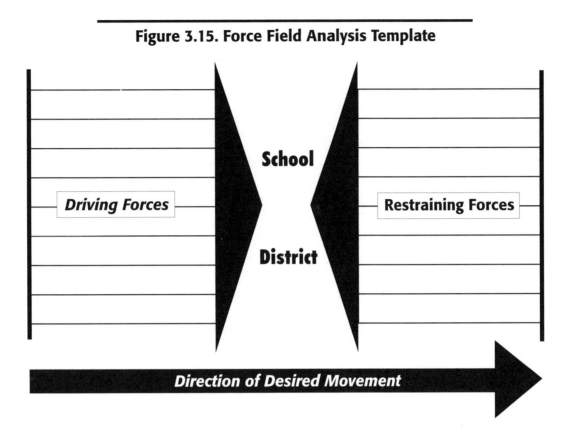

Figure 3.15. Force Field Analysis Template

Force Field Analysis can be used as a tool to brainstorm root cause hypotheses. A more sophisticated use of this tool is to assign a weight to each item based upon the team's judgment as measured through a process such as paretoing. The weighting can then be used to estimate the strength of the various forces, singly and in combination. The same weighting can be used to prioritize the forces that will be focused upon first.

In order to move the system in the direction wanted, either the driving forces have to be increased and/or the restraining forces have to be decreased. Although increasing driving forces may seem the easier to accomplish, it can often result in increased pressure on the system and even greater resistance from the restraining forces. If, on the other hand, the focus is on reducing the restraining forces, the system will move in the direction wanted without having to increase the existing driving forces. Figure 3.16 shows a completed force field constructed to review the failure of all students to achieve proficiency in mathematics.

Figure 3.16. Force Field to Review Mathematics Proficiency

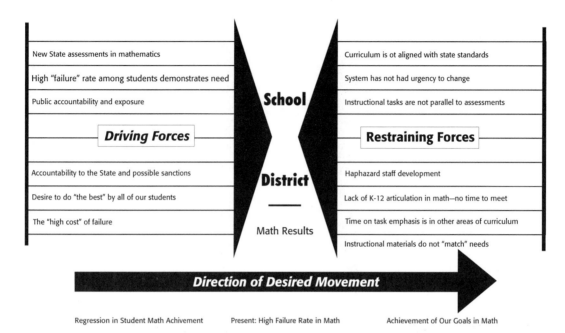

Once the hypotheses are identified, it is important that they be "proven" through analysis of data. Given the type of restraining forces identified above, many cannot be proven through the use of normal quantitative data, but instead, such tools as surveying, curriculum mapping, a tabulation of such issues as staff development training, time on task, and evaluation of materials can be used to obtain suitable data.

Once "proven" as root causes for high incidence of student failure in math, the restraining forces should become the focus of strategies to diminish their impact or to remove them completely. Likewise, driving forces should be verified, and strengthened as necessary in a manner that does not increase resistance.

When used as an RCA tool, Force Field Analysis should be facilitated in a manner that permits individual reflection, small-group discussion, and feedback to the whole of the larger group. The facilitator's guides found in the sections dealing with the Questioning Data Process and the Diagnostic Tree Process provide a model that allows this to occur.

The force field analysis template can also be used to communicate to stakeholder groups for purposes of verification and understanding of what the planning team is doing.

Presenting Root Cause Products

The RCA process needs to remain "open" and visible to all stakeholder groups. This allows for continuing suggestions and data input from as many sources as possible, as well as for verification of process results prior to implementation. It becomes the way the school goes about its work. It is therefore important that information be communicated with clarity and brevity. Brevity is necessitated by the fact that many stakeholders have only a brief amount of time to consider the work, and clarity helps to ensure understanding of what has been discovered and why.

Three types of feedback examples (Figures 3.17–3.20) are provided following their descriptions below.

Figure 3.17 (Feedback Example 1) shows how the work of the RCA or Planning Team can be shared with stakeholder groups. A copy of the June Grading Report (Figure 3.1) could be copied on its reverse side to allow for ease of reference for those wishing to examine the work in detail. Figure 3.2 (Questioning Data Schematic) could also be used as a feedback tool if the stakeholder groups become familiar with its form through regular use.

Figure 3.18 (Feedback Example 2) shows how the next level of information—What are we finding?—can be provided to stakeholder groups. It should be noted that the investigation is moving from the planning team into the departments where individual staff will discuss issues related to student failure in their courses.

In similar fashion, work completed using the Diagnostic Tree Process can be shared, perhaps most effectively by using schematics with commentary such as shown in Figure 3.9 (Extended Diagnostic Tree) and Figures 3.10–3.13 (Detailed Diagnostic Tree—Variations 1 to 4).

Figure 3.19 (Feedback Example 3) shows the flow of the Creative Root Cause Analysis process (CRCA) from beginning to implementation of strategies. The content is based upon the example used in explaining CRCA.

Another way of framing the feedback is to use a "Fishbone Diagram." The concept of the fishbone was presented by Kauro Ishikawa in 1982. The diagram is also known as an Ishikawa diagram or, sometimes, as a cause-and-effect diagram. Figure 3.20 (Feedback Example 4) shows how a fishbone can be used to simply present concepts of cause and effect. A blank template of the Fishbone Diagram (Figure 3.24) is provided in the template section of this chapter.

In addition to being a tool for communicating feedback, the Fishbone can be used as a means of guiding a brainstorming session on cause—much like the diagnostic tree. Important considerations in using it as a tool arise in properly defining the "effect" (large box), and in the use of sound facilitation techniques to obtain the maximum result from group brainstorming. Although the five major "bones" in this example have been labeled, other important factors may be identified, as alternatives or as additions.

Feedback to stakeholder groups, and communicating the root cause analysis process, can be accomplished in a great variety of ways. Feedback is not limited to the few examples shown here. The important point is to communicate consistently, briefly, and with clarity to enable conversation and to provide a response back to the team doing the work. This helps to keep the process open and the larger numbers of stakeholders informed and, perhaps, engaged as well.

Figure 3.17. Feedback Example 1

Root Cause Analysis–June Grading Report

The school comprehensive planning team has reviewed the June Grading Report and has identified six major issues reflected in the report that warrant further detailed study. We have identified the following questions regarding each of the major issues that will be researched before our next meeting.

Key Indicators of Student Success:

→ Percentage Passing All Courses
Percentage of Students Achieving Honor Roll Status
Percentage of Students on Endangered and Critical Lists

What are the six major "things" that we saw in the data?

What questions did we have about what we saw?

What are we finding?

Each of these questions will be researched and reported upon by the time of our next meeting.

- 26% of all students are on honor

  Who is, and who is not on honor roll?
  Is this normal for us? for other schools?
  What does the honor roll relate to?

- 39% of all freshmen are on either critical or endangered list.

  Who are these students?
  What programs, are they or have they been in?
  Is there a relation to discipline?

- Failure rate at the high school is 44% of all students.

  Is this normal for us? for other schools?
  Who are these students?
  Where and why are they failing?

- Over 12% of students fail three or more courses.

  What are the courses most often failed?
  What are the reasons for the failures?
  What do these students think?

- Seniors account for fewer failures.

  Why?
  What has been the dropout rate?
  Is this normal for us? for other schools?

- 52% of all freshmen failed at least one course.

  Who are these freshmen?
  Where did they fail?
  Why did they fail?

If you have suggestions, or additional data, that you wish to share with the planning team please give them to your representative.

Figure 3.18. Feedback Example 2

Root Cause Analysis–June Grading Report

The school comprehensive planning team has reviewed the June Grading Report and has identified six major issues reflected in the report that warrant further detailed study. The questions below either have been researched or are still in the process of being researched. What we have found to date is presented in the third (right) column.

Key Indicators of Student Success: → Percentage Passing All Courses
Percentage of Students Achieving Honor Roll Status
Percentage of Students on Endangered and Critical Lists

What are the six major "things" that we saw in the data?	What questions did we have about what we saw?	What are we finding?
26% of all students are on honor roll.	Who is, and who is not on honor roll? Is this normal for us? for other schools? What does the honor roll relate to?	Most of those on honor roll are female and in the academic track. It is normal for us, but not for most other schools. Being female, college bound, and having high grades.
39% of all freshmen are on either critical or endangered list.	Who are these students? What programs, are they or have they been in? Is there a relation to discipline?	Most of these are male local diploma students. Although there are some special needs students, they are not a large proportion of the group. Many of these students have been, or are, in remedial programs. Yes. Most discipline incidents are related to local diploma male students.
Failure rate at the high school is 44% of all students.	Is this normal for us? for other schools? Who are these students? Where and why are they failing?	It is normal for us, but for none of the other five high schools studied. Their failure rates range from 33% to 17%. Again, the largest group of failing students are the male, local diploma students. Departments with the highest failure rates in relation to enrollment are: Social Studies (23%), Science (27%), and Technology Education (36%). The school average failure rate is 17%. The team has studied the specific courses where there are high rates of failure, and departments are preparing information as to what they see as the reason. Students will also be asked to identify reasons for their failure. This phase of the root cause analysis is continuing.

What are the six major "things" that we saw in the data?	What questions did we have about what we saw?	What are we finding?
■ Over 12% of students fail three or more courses.	What are the courses most often failed?	This information will become more clear when the analysis above is completed. Most often, however, the failures are in local diploma classes.
	What are the reasons for the failures?	See above.
	What do these students think?	See above.
■ Seniors account for fewer failures.	Why?	Not determined at this time.
	What has been the dropout rate?	4.5% annually.
	Is this normal for us? for other schools?	Normal for us, but higher than other schools.
■ 52% of all freshmen failed at least one course.	Who are these freshmen?	Largely local diploma male students.
	Where did they fail?	See above.
	Why did they fail?	See above—continuing analysis.

This is preliminary feedback of our first findings regarding the three key indicators of student success as reported by the June Grading Report. The analysis is continuing at the department and student levels. Detailed data tables in support of the findings are available in the faculty room, school library, and department offices. Individual copies may be obtained by request.

Figure 3.19. Feedback Example 3

Creative Root Cause Analysis Process

Probing Question 1:

Why is there lack of statewide clarity on the concept and utilization of comprehensive planning as a tool to increase student achievement and district effectiveness?

Individual Answers Grouped by Categories:*

- ◆ Comprehensive Planning Pilot Project Infrastructure and Logistics

  - Inability to easily resolve issue of including all other required plans in this plan

  - Lack of clarity on comprehensive planning process

  - Lack of a fully formed comprehensive planning process

  - Not enough skilled facilitators to do comprehensive planning in all districts

  - It is a big and diverse state

  - Tools are not available to support in-depth data analysis

  - Facilitator confusion on how to best approach districts

  - Unsophisticated comprehensive planning pilot infrastructure

  - Lack of a research base

  - Facilitator "role confusion"—facilitation vs. consultation

  - Malformed comprehensive planning pilot infrastructure

  - Comprehensive planning model is rather complex with a different theoretical base

  - Clarity and simplicity in comprehensive planning publications

  - Lack of a marketing plan

  - Lack of plan to get the State Education Department (SED) on board

- ◆ School Culture

  - Competing district agendas

  - Lack of district leadership and support for comprehensive planning

  - Lack of Board of Education support and understanding

  - Lack of parental support and understanding

- Comprehensive planning requires "rethinking" of the planning process
- Facilitators are not familiar with individual district culture
- Lack of systems training
- Lack of adequate time to do comprehensive planning
- Current district structures do not support comprehensive planning process
- Districts may already have a planning process that they do not want to leave

♦ Understanding the Comprehensive Planning Model

- Districts do not understand the comprehensive planning model and how it can help focus district resources on student achievement
- Competing regional support agency agendas
- Facilitators need uniform training

♦ The State Education Department

- SED has not used comprehensive planning themselves
- Lack of a comprehensive planning "champion" within SED
- SED reliance on current procedures and plans
- SED is isolated and territorial
- Competing priorities and agendas on part of SED staff
- Lack of internal communication among all levels at SED
- Lack of understanding at highest levels of SED as to how comprehensive planning can act as a vehicle for current SED initiatives
- SED does not have "action plan" for implementation of comprehensive planning
- Ambiguous SED policy statements
- Needed assurances from SED that comprehensive planning process will meet requirements for other plans
- SED structure and individual actions continue to be based upon old role of watchdog

♦ Understanding the Concept of Systems

- Lack of systems training - understanding of systems

*Categories were developed based upon the individual answers to the probing question above.

Probing Question 2:

What are the major roots underlying most of the issues identified above over which we have control?

- ◆ Answers arrived at using both the team problem-solving process and the team communication cycle in CRCA:

  - Lack of clarity, simplicity, and uniformity in publications and materials

  - Inadequate infrastructure for dissemination of training

  - Lack of an effective means of communicating to all involved

  - Incomplete training for everyone, particularly facilitators of the process

- ◆ Suggested strategies to resolve major roots listed above:

  - Establishing a comprehensive planning facilitators academy that would "teach" a curriculum designed to provide uniform understanding and skills in support of the comprehensive planning pilot.

  - Developing enhanced but simplified uniform support materials for facilitators, school districts, and those interested in learning more.

  - Strengthening the infrastructure of the comprehensive planning team through more regular meetings, a listserv, and Web site.

  - Expanding membership in the steering committee to include greater diversity of representation.

  - Seeking out a high-level leader within the state education department as a project "champion".

Suggested strategies are to be discussed, and if approved, implemented through development and carrying out of action plans

Figure 3.20. Feedback Example 4

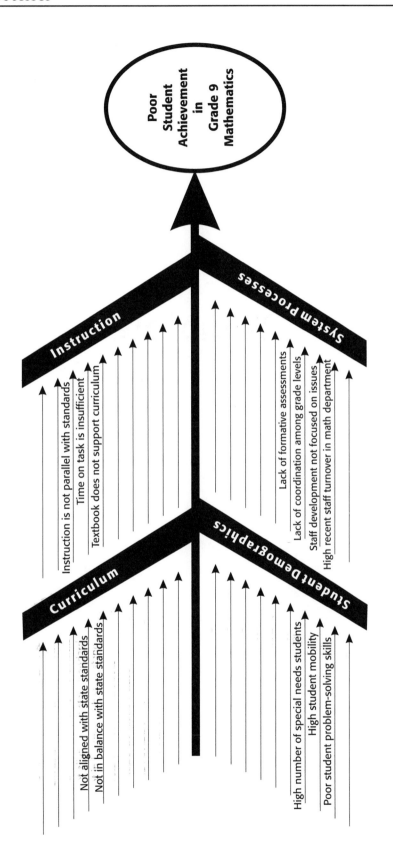

Templates

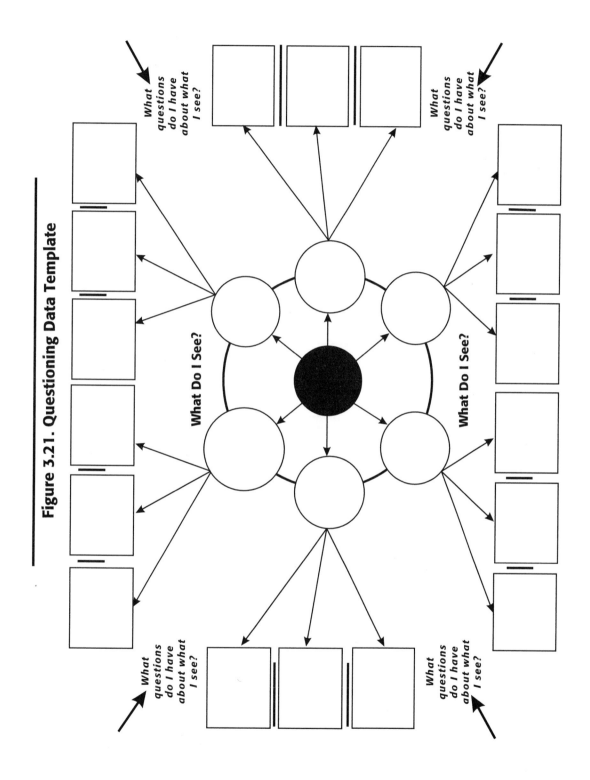

Figure 3.21. Questioning Data Template

Figure 3.22. Questioning Data Template—Outline Format

What data set is being used? _____

For what purpose? _____

What do I "see" in the data?

    1. _____

    2. _____

    3. _____

    4. _____

    5. _____

    6. _____

What questions do I have about what I "see" in the data?

    a. _____

    b. _____

    c. _____

    d. _____

    e. _____

    f. _____

    g. _____

    h. _____

    i. _____

    j. _____

    k. _____

Figure 3.23. The Diagnostic Tree Template

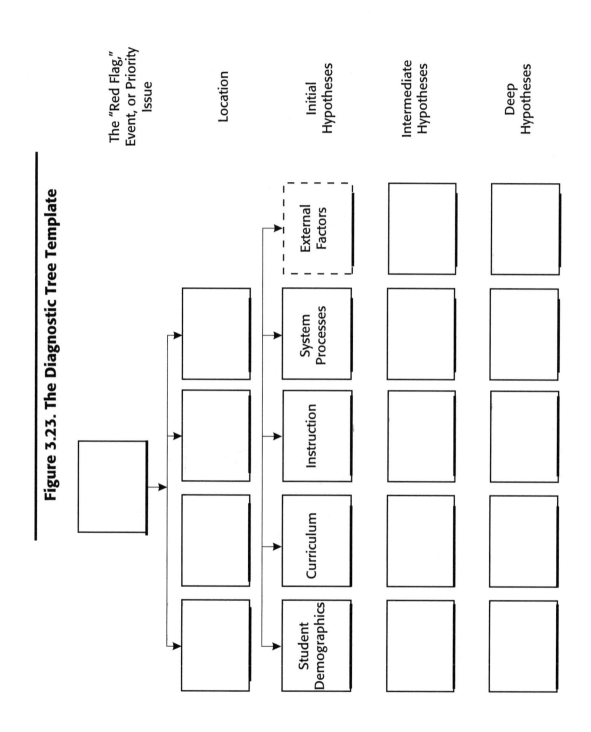

The "Red Flag," Event, or Priority Issue

Location

Initial Hypotheses

Intermediate Hypotheses

Deep Hypotheses

External Factors

System Processes

Instruction

Curriculum

Student Demographics

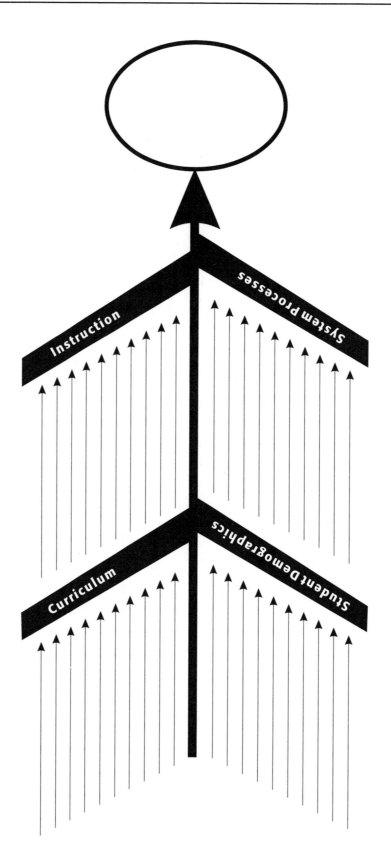

Figure 3.24. Fishbone Diagram Template

Summary

This chapter began with an overview of observations regarding problems associated with the developing use of data in schools, and suggested remedies for each were presented. Data is central to effective root cause analysis. The observations and suggested remedies need to be taken seriously in order to develop the data infrastructure essential for sound root cause analysis.

The following five processes for seeking root cause were described, and examples of each were given:

1. Questioning Data

2. The Diagnostic Tree

3. Creative Root Cause Analysis

4. The Five Whys

5. Force Field Analysis

A school district team may choose to use all of these processes, depending upon the issue at hand, or concentrate on the use of one or two as a means of building consistency and understanding among stakeholder groups.

It is important that a root cause analysis process remain open. This means that it is not done in secret, nor are the results "sprung" on surprised stakeholders. Rather, verification of the team's work and stakeholder input and response is sought as the process unfolds. Frequent, brief, clear communications encourage this to occur. Various formats for communication to stakeholder groups regarding the progress and products of the team were presented, and templates of these formats were provided.

4

Using
Root Cause Analysis

But I have observed that the districts with the most tightly aligned and data-driven approaches to change and improvement are also those making a difference in student achievement.

Edie L. Holcomb, *Getting Excited about Data*

Where Does Root Cause Analysis Fit?

Root Cause Analysis (RCA) should be used anytime one wants to discover the causes for success or eliminate the causes of a "red-flag" issue. Root cause analysis should be the underlying thought process used in all problem solving and discovery. The context can be an individual teacher working within the limits of a single classroom and single group of students, or it can be a district-wide team of stakeholders seeking the most fundamental causes for a system-wide gap in achievement. Recalling the four modalities of root cause analysis, the context can be either proactive or reactive and it can focus upon causes for success or failure.

Although this guide focuses primarily on issues related to student achievement outcomes in the negative reactive mode, root cause analysis can be used for any process and in any mode. "All work is process." Root cause analysis therefore can be used to determine why it takes so long to process purchase orders or why the cafeteria program is so successful, as well as for discovering why student learning is not up to expectations. It can be used to learn why certain programs are successful and how those elements of success might be applied to new initiatives. Root cause analysis is a way of thinking as much as it is a structured problem-solving and discovery process.

Two Nonacademic Examples

Example 1

A high school was dissatisfied with how lunch time feeding of students was carried out. It seemed that "cafeteria" caused numerous disciplinary, attitudinal, and school climate problems. The lunch periods seemed to have the greatest negative impact on the afternoon session of school. A group of cafeteria and instructional staff was convened with selected students to review the situation and to make recommendations. Upon studying the situation the following issues were identified:

- The cafeteria could only hold one-third of the students, thereby necessitating three cafeteria periods—covering one-third of the day.

- Serving lines (only two) were limited, causing a long wait time in line.

- Menu selection was limited because there were only two serving lines.

- Students were seated at long, trough-like rows of tables with little space between.

- The three cafeteria periods ran one after the other with no time to clean tables, floors, or waste barrels between periods.

- Rest rooms were not available, nor were pay phones, so students had to leave the cafeteria to make use of either.

An opportunity to resolve many of these casual factors came with a building project. Through the project, the following modifications were made:

- The cafeteria was doubled in size.

- Rest rooms and pay phones were installed within the area of the cafeteria.

- Serving lines were doubled to four, enabling a salad bar and fast food line in addition to the regular school lunch lines.

- All seating was either in booths or square or round tables of four.

- The ambiance of the cafeteria was changed from "institutional" to "fast food Americana" complete with outside walled patio and sun room treatment of the two exterior walls.

In addition, while keeping the three lunch periods, the school altered its master schedule to allow for a ten minute "vacant time" between each of the sessions. This provided adequate time for custodial and cafeteria staff to empty waste barrels, clean tables, and sweep floors so that each new group of students would be presented with a freshened environment.

Result:

Problems associated with the cafeteria decreased dramatically, afternoon sessions of the school were improved, cafeteria disciplinary referrals decreased, participation increased, and satisfaction increased.

Comments:

In effect, this was a rather simple and unsophisticated root cause analysis process. The use of data, except for experiential data of the committee, was limited. However, the group sought to eliminate, or dissolve roots, rather than impose patches (more supervisory staff, more rules, firmer discipline and consequences) on the already overburdened system.

Example 2

A vocational high school serving 12 member school districts was experiencing a higher rate of disciplinary infractions than desired. A thorough analysis of each incident over the course of the preceding year was conducted. This consisted of identification of each incident by: type of incident, location or source, student demographic data, sending school district, and sending teacher, if any. The analysis revealed that students from certain school districts were more likely to be involved in disciplinary incidents than students from other school districts. The analysis also revealed that as many as one-third of the incidents were related to issues of transportation. Students were: driving to the school without permission, transporting other students without permission, or getting into trouble while waiting for their bus to return home. Again, the majority of these incidents involved students from three districts that did not run a special bus to pick up the morning students. These students had to wait an hour at the vocational center for the afternoon students to arrive, and then ride that bus back to their home district. Instead of waiting the hour, many drove without permission, or transported their friends. Others got into trouble while waiting. This analysis of the data was used as a tool in working with the home districts to reduce the problems caused by the lack of timely bussing. The analysis also revealed the need to work with specific individual school districts on the need for greater cooperation in dealing with disciplinary incidents. Finally, there was also a pattern of disciplinary issues within and among the vocational staff that identified the need for staff discussion and potential conferencing with, or training of, individual teachers.

Comments:

The quantification of the disciplinary data enabled the administration to "chunk" the various sources of disciplinary incidents within the school. Once the sources were identified, causes were easier to find. The data supplied the necessary facts to explain the issues to faculty and to initiate discussions with member school districts. The analysis provided support for the strategic steps recommended to reduce the perceived high level of disciplinary incidents within the school.

Two Academic Examples

Example 3

A large, urban, high school has a high degree of failure in a required ninth-grade math course. A state examination was conducted at the end of the course in June. There was a high failure rate for both the course and the examination.

Three groups of students were identified and studied:

1. Students who passed the course and who passed the state exam.

2. Students who passed the course and who failed the state exam.

3. Students who failed the course and who failed the state exam.

For some reason, perhaps lack of numbers, a fourth group, those who failed the course but passed the state exam, was not studied.

Teacher-given grades for each of the three groups were plotted. Although for all three groups the first quarter grade was typically the highest (an interesting factor that should have been investigated further), the second quarter grades for students who were destined to fail both the course and the exam dropped drastically. In fact, it was felt that students who were to fail the exam and the course could be identified as early as the 10th week of school, yet nothing significantly different was being offered to these students.

Multiple questions and areas of thought emerged in discussions with the math department. Were these students misplaced? Should there be another course offering, perhaps an extended course, that would better enable them to achieve success? Where were these students last year, and the year before? Can we identify them earlier than the 10th week of the ninth grade? What can we do once they are identified at the 10th week or 20th week? Can we restructure the school to provide these students with additional help or time, or must they continue their 30-week walk to predictable failure? Can we learn anything from the students who passed the course and the exam? Would an item analysis of the exam as well as an analysis of the reasons for course failure be productive?

Comments:

Although this example does not conclude with a happy ending for all, as the process is still under way, it is evident that the process of root cause analysis opens up deep avenues into the organization and structure of the school and asks questions regarding what needs to be changed to enable the targeted group of students to succeed. It is also obvious that this is a systems issue more than a high school issue. Although certain organizational and programmatic issues can be dealt with at the high school, the roots for ninth-grade unpreparedness and failure go down into the preceding grades and buildings.

Example 4

Another large, urban, high school had a high dropout rate. In fact, the rate was sufficiently high to warrant state identification as a school in need of improvement. A planning committee of more than 40 people was assembled to investigate possible causes and strategies to improve the situation.

They identified the following major issues:

♦ The school operated an open campus, and its 2400 students liberally took advantage of the fact to stay away from school, particularly in the afternoons.

♦ Many students cut classes and hung out in nearby malls.

♦ The school district had a 13/26 attendance policy that required students who missed more than 13 days of class within a single semester to drop the course. More than 26 absences in a year resulted in dropping the course as well.

♦ The school was designed for 1500 students and enrollment was 2400.

♦ Instructional programs were not enticing.

Change strategies included:

♦ Closing the campus—all students remained within the building.

♦ Implemented a "truancy retrieval system" that consisted of truant officers and a bus that made regular trips to the local malls.

♦ Dropped the 13/26 rule as school policy.

♦ Floated a bond, with public approval, for additions to the school to bring capacity up to enrollment

♦ Built a "pavilion" that is similar to a mall food court where students can go during out-of-class time.

♦ Divided the large (2400) high school into four schools within a school.

♦ Worked at making instruction more enticing.

Results:

Greatly reduced dropout rate and removal from state list of schools in need of improvement.

Comments:

This is an obvious case where the root causes are multiple and intertwined. Working on any one root separately would not have brought about the desired results. It was necessary, therefore, to identify and attack all of the major roots at the same time.

In each of these cases, the committees working on the problem did not jump from problem to solution, nor did they attempt to patch the situation by applying remedies to the symptoms. In each case the committee working on the problem attempted to reveal, as best as it was able, the underlying causes of the problem, and its strategies were aimed at the causes—not the problem.

Chapter 6 contains additional examples of root cause analysis taken from a wide variety of contexts. Once one becomes sensitive to the concept of root cause, it is difficult to find a morning edition of nearly any paper that does not contain at least one news item where root cause analysis is at work. In order to continually improve student learning, schools must learn to solve their problems and reach their decisions using the set of concepts and skills that are called root cause analysis.

Systems Planning

One of the most powerful contexts for root cause analysis is found within a whole system planning process. Often, school systems and planning teams jump from problem to solution without ever considering why the problem exists in the first place or considering what forces are restraining the system from accomplishing its goals. Figure 4.1 illustrates steps in such a typical whole system planning process.

Figure 4.1 A Typical Planning Process

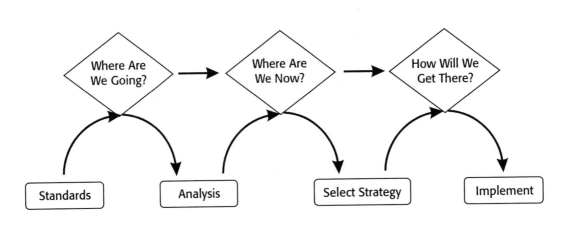

This typical approach to planning, or problem solving, asks only three questions:

1. *Where are we going?* This is answered by defining local and state standards in terms of key indicators of student success that include a means of measurement.

2. *Where are we now?* This is found by analysis of relatively simple Level One data—the measurements of key indicators of student success.

3. *How will we get there?* Unfortunately, the answer to this question is often based on uninformed opinion or "knee-jerk" reaction rather than on data. Strategies for "getting there" are not measured against forces that are restraining the effort. Strategies for getting there are frequently aimed at the symptoms rather than the causes. The solutions implemented by such a process are therefore patches on symptoms—like buckets placed under leaking pipes.

Many efforts at improving learning are also confined to the teacher, department, or building that initiated them rather than including the whole system.

In a systems approach to planning and problem solving, an additional step is added to the traditional process, and it is understood that causes will be sought, no matter if they are beyond the "walls" of the unit that initiated the process. This is why it is essential that all school improvement efforts be linked to a district-wide planning effort. A systems approach is shown in Figure 4.2.

Figure 4.2. A Systems Planning Process

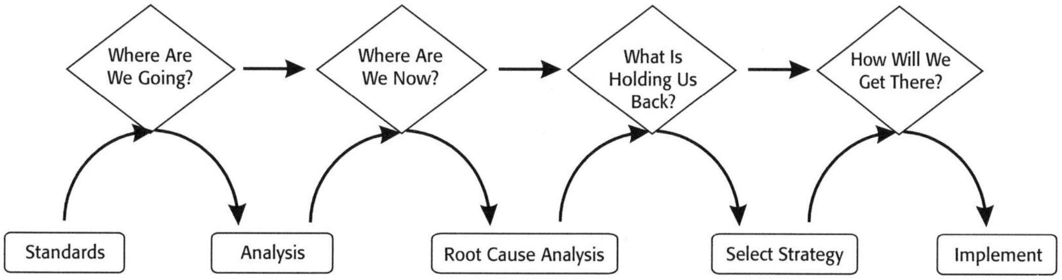

Root Cause Analysis brings about an investigative pause in the process that enables the discovery of underlying reasons for the problem or gap, which in turn enables the solution to be focused on eliminating the causes for the problem rather than on covering over its symptoms. The underlying reasons, or causes, must be sought throughout the system rather than just in the process under study. A middle school, for example, that is seeking causes for high levels of student failure in grade 8 math, should not limit its analysis to factors only within its grade 6–8 structure but should follow where the data leads—even into the elementary grades. Likewise, district processes, such as staff development, staffing, textbook selection, and funding, should also be part of the investigation if it is demonstrated that they are possible causes for the problem.

The goals and strategies identified through the planning process must be monitored and evaluated on a regular basis. Monitoring is checking to ensure that "we are doing what we said we would do," whereas evaluating is measuring to see if what we are doing is "making a difference" in moving the system towards its goals. Each Board of Education meeting should have a segment devoted to both monitoring and evaluation of the plan, and the plan itself should be the primary agenda for the school leadership team. Otherwise the whole planning effort, as well as the root cause analysis, soon becomes a "sidecar issue" rather than the way the school intends to conduct its business.

RCA and Required Planning Processes

Many states and larger school districts require some form of comprehensive school-wide improvement planning. This is more than just a national concern, given that one can easily find examples of required educational planning processes around the world. In some instances, all schools within a jurisdiction are required to complete and to submit such plans, whereas in others, it is only required of high-need or low-performing districts. In a few instances, the jurisdiction has wisely seen fit to make the plan district-wide rather than simply building-focused. Invariably, however, the required planning models omit or provide only scant mention of the concept of root cause analysis. Indeed, one unidentified state includes the following in its guidelines for analyzing data (out of fear that a casual reader would mistake the "What to Do's" and "What Not to Do's" above as advice contained in this guide, an "author's critique" has been added to identify correct from erroneous guidance):

		Author's Critique
1) What to do:		
A)	Identify strengths and weaknesses	OK
B)	State only what the data says	Wrong
C)	Focus on student related information	OK
2) What not to do:		
A)	Do not offer solutions in findings	OK
B)	Do not describe cause or blame in findings	Wrong
C)	Do not include wishes or wants in findings	OK

The same guidelines then go on to suggest the following "Questions to answer when planning:"

1. Where are we?

2. Where do we want to go? What goal do we want to reach?

3. What will it look like when we get there?

4. What do we need to get there?

5. How will we know if we get there?

6. What changes will we make if we don't get to our destination?

Stating only what the data says seems simple and direct enough until one thinks just a bit more deeply. Data typically says little. Although we often use the term "data" in such expressions as, "If you do not have data you are just a person with an opinion" (Deming), data needs to be analyzed in the context of other measures and over time. Many factors need to be brought into the discussion in order to convert raw data into information, knowledge, understanding, and wisdom.

Not identifying blame is fine—school improvement will not occur when fingers are pointed in all directions ascribing blame. But not to seek cause is an abdication of responsibility. How can one begin to answer planning question 4, "What do we need to get there?" unless one has a very good idea of what the cause for not getting there is? How does one select strategies for improvement without knowing how one needs to improve?

The Department of Education of Western Australia has a planning process that is focused on improved student outcomes, and on reporting student performance to parents, the community, and to the Education Department. This process of planning and accountability is described on its Web site as consisting of three major elements that appear to be so general that they offer scant direction to those sincerely seeking to make a difference for students. The most positive aspect of the elements described, however, are that they are not restrictive and that they provide ample room for local creativity and skill. Figure 4.3 indicates how root cause analysis "fits" into the relatively open planning construct presented in Western Australia.

Figure 4.3. Government of Western Australia, Department of Education: Planning for Improved Student Outcomes

Government of Western Australia Accountability Planning	Author's Suggestions and Commentary
Identify the outcomes sought	Each school must identify its own "Key Indicators for Success," some of which are most likely mandated by the state, whereas others may be strictly local in origin. Once agreed upon, key indicators are used to identify strengths and weaknesses and to quantify and prioritize gaps in student performance. See Chapter 2.
Collect information about the extent to which these outcomes are being achieved.	This element should include the following steps: • Collecting the data (measurements of key indicators) • Analysis of Level One data to identify gaps in achievement • Prioritizing the gap areas to identify the most significant
Insert root cause analysis	After the gaps have been prioritized, seek cause for priority gaps using root cause analysis tools.
Take appropriate action to ensure that students experience success in achieving outcomes	Again, this element consists of a number of essential steps: • Select strategies to dissolve identified root causes • Develop action plans for each strategyImplement action plans • Monitor Implementation—Are we doing what we said we would do? • Evaluate results—Did it make a difference?

The British Columbia Ministry of Education requires all schools to establish school planning councils that include parents beginning with the 2002–2003 school year. Interim guidelines for the first year of implementation indicate that the plans developed by these councils should focus on student achievement in the areas of intellectual, human, social, and career development, and that the plans should be student-focused and sensitive to the full range of students being served. Planning includes a goal-setting process that is very similar to the identification of Key Indicators of Student Success, as well as the use of a variety of data to assess achievement of goals. As fine as the interim guidelines are, however, they do not sufficiently address the need for discovering cause, and, therefore, are enabling school planning councils to commit the fatal flaw of jumping from problem to solution. Like many other planning processes, British Columbia's has ample room for inserting root cause analysis. In this case, this opportunity occurs within the very first step, which is identified as "Collecting and Interpreting Student Performance Data."

The State of Vermont's "Action Planning" is a well-developed process that has been required for several years. One step in the process is identified as "Hypothesize Causes," which is followed by "Look Deeper at Other Measures and Indicators." The RCA tools and processes suggested in this guide fit well into these two steps. Figure 4.4 (page 118) presents a rough overview of the steps in Vermont's "Action Planning," along with the author's suggestions and commentary.

The State of Maryland's "School Improvement Planning" (SIP) process is an excellent example of a highly developed process supported by an equally developed Web site complete with detailed tutorials. Their school improvement planning Web pages can be found at www.msde.state.md.us. One of the 10 steps in Maryland's process is identified as "Clarifying the Problem." In this step, Maryland's State Department of Education has listed the following Key Actions and Key Questions:

Key Actions:

♦ Collect additional data about your instructional program based on priority questions.

♦ Hypothesize root causes and contributing factors for why your data looks like it does.

♦ Collect evidence to prove or disprove selected hypotheses.

♦ Collect input from major stakeholders during this process.

♦ Identify a small number of high-impact causes to address in the school improvement plan.

Key Questions:

♦ Why does the data look like it does?

♦ What are the root causes and contributing factors of the data results?

♦ What does our instructional program look like in the identified testing area?

♦ Do all staff know what and how state assessments assess and what a good response looks like?

♦ Do staff teach and assess the indicators being tested in state assessments?

♦ How do staff monitor individual student progress on the indicators?

♦ How do staff intervene with students not demonstrating proficiency?"

Figure 4.4. Vermont's Action Planning Process:
Importance of Key Indicators and Root Cause Analysis

State of Vermont Action Planning	*Author's Suggestions and Commentary*
Collect and Organize Data	Dr. Victoria Bernhardt's concept of "multiple measures" of data reminds us that all types of data should be considered. This includes not only student achievement data, but student demographic data, school system process data and stakeholder perceptive data as well.
Examine Student Performance Data	Each school must identify its own "Key Indicators for Success," some of which are most likely mandated by the state, whereas others may be strictly local in origin. Once agreed upon, key indicators are used to identify strengths and weaknesses and to quantify and prioritize gaps in student performance.
Identify Strengths and Weaknesses Based on Student Performance Data	Standard Gap Analysis and identification of areas of success.
Look at Equity as Well as Excellence	Process of disaggregation of student key indicator
Hypothesize Causes	The key to successful search for cause is the use of a Root Cause Analysis (RCA) based upon data disaggregation and deeper analysis. This helps to eliminate unfounded opinion, prejudice, and organizational myth. RCA also reduces false starts, patching of symptoms, and waste of scarce resources. Data must be converted to information, knowledge, understanding, and wisdom. Hopefully, data-based decisions can be made at the level of understanding and wisdom.
Look Deeper at Other Measures and Indicators	
Formulate Actions	Action planning should not be an "add-on activity" but rather the way the school conducts its business. The Action Plan is not "shelf art," it is the plan of activities for the school in much the same way that a curriculum should guide instruction. Action planning is not an outrigger event; it is the core around which all other plans and activities of the school must revolve.
Set Initial Performance Targets	These should be based upon the identified Key Indicators of Student Success.
Set Priorities	

Maryland's School Improvement Planning process also incorporates such elements as "verification" of root cause factors identified by the planning team through what they call "peer review." Maryland's SIP process is obviously meant to be open and one that seeks discussion and input regarding its findings.

Figure 4.5 (page 120) demonstrates how RCA is a key element in New York's Comprehensive District Education Planning pilot process (CDEP). Although root cause analysis was included in CDEP by design, RCA can be easily "inserted" as a basic step in any required planning process. It is impossible to visualize an improvement process that does not have room to consider forces holding the school back from accomplishing its goals.

From just this brief exploration of several sample planning processes, several things become evident. First, the need for educational planning and for educational planning processes appears to be widespread, across state and even international boundaries. Second, there is wide diversity in how this need is being addressed. Some jurisdictions require planning, whereas in others it is optional. Some planning processes are highly detailed with much supporting materials, whereas others are relatively ill-defined with little detailed supporting materials. In at least one jurisdiction, the process appears to negate the need to find cause. Third, nearly all planning processes either explicitly suggest the need to seek root cause, or provide ample flexibility to include the search for cause within its process. Finally, it is the primary premise of this guide that the quality of results from all school improvement processes, regardless of their name or the number of steps into which they have been divided, will be substantially improved through the use of an intentional search for cause. This is true for improvement efforts in all areas of school operations, whether they be focused on academic achievement or not.

Figure 4.5. A Comprehensive Planning Process

Based upon New York's Comprehensive District Education Planning Pilot Project

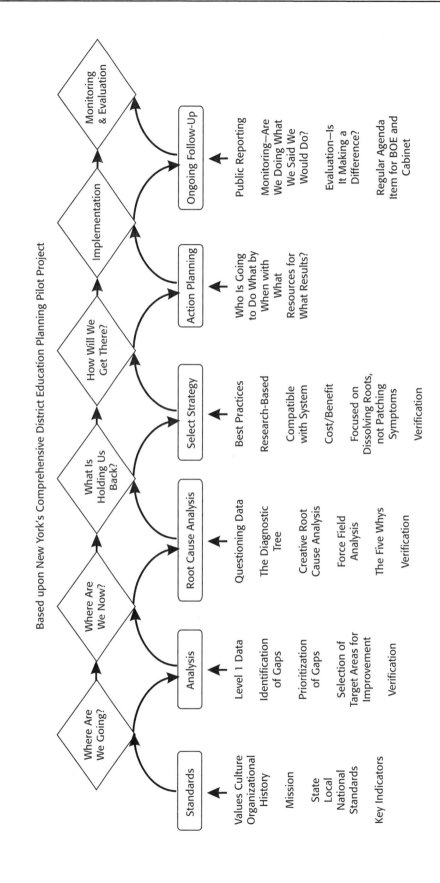

Summary

Root Cause Analysis "fits" anytime one wants to discover causes for success or eliminate causes for failure. Although the most frequent modality for RCA is in the negative reactive mode—seeking what went wrong—it also can, and should be, used more frequently to learn from what went right. RCA can also be used proactively to either remove obstacles or to implant necessary elements prior to implementation of new programs.

Root Cause Analysis can be used in all types of academic and nonacademic problem-solving situations. It can be used by a single teacher seeking to improve classroom issues, or by a department, team, or building. Its greatest power, however, is when it is used within a system-wide context, because roots are sometimes located far from the symptom.

Typical planning processes often jump from problem to solution without considering cause for the problem. Solutions should be designed to dissolve causes, not patch over symptoms.

The concept of school improvement planning has spread widely across the United States, and, indeed, is international in scope. Individual school jurisdictions have also developed a variety of school improvement planning processes. Although at this stage of their development few include the specific concepts associated with RCA, nearly all have elements that permit or even encourage digging deeply into the data prior to reaching decisions. All school improvement planning processes can be improved through the use of an intentional and systematic search for cause.

5
Considerations

If schools are to change, it must first be understood that it is not enough to change the behavior of individuals—what must be changed as well are the systems that encourage, support, and maintain present behavior patterns and discourage new patterns from emerging.

Phillip C. Schlecty, *Inventing Better Schools*

How to Use This Chapter

Although this chapter is in the middle of the guide, it was actually the last one written, so, in its own way, it is a type of reservoir of final thoughts and suggestions. It was the most difficult chapter to assemble, and was even more difficult to conclude because the conversation on these issues is ongoing, developmental, and never ending.

Each section in this chapter is actually a "stand-alone" piece. However, each piece is also a fragment of the whole that is being conveyed. You will find multiple strands of thought in this chapter that are also woven into other chapters of this guide. Of all the chapters, this one points most forcefully to the larger need for organizational change in schools, as opposed to the use of RCA with a much more limited function.

The final three sections deal with fundamental understandings necessary for successful analysis of root cause: systems thinking, data, and variation.

It is hoped that the thoughts presented in this chapter will encourage the reader's reflection on how they apply to their own unique setting. Paul Houston's thoughts, reproduced below, challenge us to think and act holistically, rather than in parts:

> While top-down reform has its place and bottom-up reform has its merits, something must connect the two, and that something is the system. Education is a living, breathing organism that cannot be taken apart or fixed in pieces, as one might fix a mechanical apparatus. It is organic and must be improved systematically. All the parts

must be attended to and that is the role of school systems and school system leaders."

Paul D. Houston, AASA Executive Director. (1998, September). *The School Administrator, 55*(8), p. 53.

The Issue of Leadership

Because this is a "school leader's" guide to root cause analysis, it is appropriate to explore the issue of leadership as it relates to school improvement and the search for root cause. For purposes of this discussion, two aspects of school leadership have been identified—(a) central leadership and (b) distributed leadership.

Central Leadership

Central Leadership is leadership emanating from traditional positional authority. In schools, these positions are the superintendent, key assistants, principals and various program coordinators, directors, and chairs. Work with schools in New York State and the comprehensive planning process indicates that one cannot have a successful comprehensive plan without committed and visibly involved central leadership. At the district level, this is focused on the position of superintendent of schools, whereas at the building level, staff must see the principal as engaged in, supportive of, and highly committed to the process. Although assistants can carry the primary load of maintaining or moving the process along, only the CEO can provide the *imprimatur* that this is the way "we will do our business." This is just as true of root cause analysis as it is for action or comprehensive planning.

Central leaders are responsible for:

♦ Establishing an organizational culture and system capacity that support the use of data and the analysis of causes for problems and successes.

♦ Implementing processes that staff will regularly use to seek cause rather than allowing the patching of problems.

♦ Implementing the action plan that develops from all root cause analysis process.

♦ Requiring continuous monitoring of action plans and evaluation of student results.

Distributed Leadership

Today's schools are also moving to various forms of shared leadership and decision making. In New York State, for example, Commissioner's Regulation 100.11 requires shared decision making at the building level by councils representative of major stakeholder groups such as staff, parents, community, and administration. In many states and provinces, similar initiatives have taken hold. Increasingly, schools and districts encourage leadership to become distributed by design with different people playing leadership roles at different times depending upon the issue at hand. Teachers are now being called upon in ways that might not have been imagined 10 or 15 years ago. These new roles include teachers as:

♦ Mentors

♦ Trainers

♦ Leaders of meaningful committees

♦ Curricular specialists serving a dual instructional/administrative role

Although this process is by no means complete, and its strength varies by district, there is no mistaking the general trend toward greater participation, involvement, and power on the part of instructional staff in decision making.

This distribution of leadership will continue and expand in the years ahead as the role of teacher changes from that of an isolated professional to that of an active and informed participant in the decision-making process. The rigid hierarchical structure of the past can no longer successfully deal with the myriad challenges facing public education's future. Such distributed leadership does not negate the importance of central office commitment to continuous school improvement using root cause analysis, but rather strengthens the capacity of school districts to make use of it.

With distributed leadership, however, we must deal with the need for widespread understanding and skill in the analysis and use of data for seeking root cause. All staff must have an underlying concept of systems and be able to "see" systems and processes alive in their school context. They must understand variation. They must form the habit of seeking the reasons underlying the problem rather than grasping for patches to place on symptoms. This can all be accomplished through specific training, reading, and practice that are enmeshed within the ongoing local school improvement process.

Central leaders must actively demonstrate their understanding and commitment in such ways as to enable an organizational culture in which distributed leadership can flourish, and then use this newly developed capacity for the continuous improvement of student learning.

Distributed leaders must be aligned with the school's specific learning goals, learn the skills, and assume shared responsibility for moving the system forward.

Contexts for RCA

Root cause analysis can be used at any level within a school district or building, as the following examples illustrate:

♦ A teacher working to improve classroom instruction.

♦ A work group charged with the responsibility of solving a singular problem or issue.

♦ A grade level or department seeking to improve learning.

♦ A committee or team charged with the overall responsibility for school improvement.

♦ A district planning council seeking to remove local barriers to student success on a district level.

Root cause analysis also can be used to discover the underlying causes for failure in any process—not just academic achievement.

In each of these instances, all four root cause modalities can be utilized, although the emphasis is usually on "negative reactive" analysis. The comments that follow are pertinent to all levels and processes, no matter which modality is employed.

The key to all successful root cause analysis is to start with data. No doubt, it was some sort of data that indicated a problem in the first place. Now, the same data have to be used again—this time to dig deeply using the processes described in Chapter 3. Data are most useful when they can be converted to information, knowledge, understanding, and wisdom. Professional opinion and judgment are most useful when informed and supported by data.

Because most of the people involved in root cause analysis also have full-time responsibilities as teachers, administrators, students, or, perhaps, as working citizens, it is important that the setting include supporting resources. Generally, it is too much to expect that the committee, group, or individual teacher will be able to gather the data, analyze the data, and make use of the data. Committees, groups, and teachers should be supplied key data elements in an easy-to-understand form. Preliminary analysis of the data should also be provided. This requires the assignment of human resources to complete these tasks in the intervals between meetings of the team.

Schools now have to be as interested in data about student learning as they have been in data about dollars. Schools will have to create and maintain data warehouses containing information about student learning. The "No Child Left Behind" legislation makes this a necessity. The data in such warehouses must be converted to information, knowledge, understanding, and wisdom before they can be used for decision making.

Although many school districts are moving rapidly in this direction, most current committees have scant support in their data retrieval and analysis efforts. In the interim, it is essential that a key administrative person, assisted by clerical help, "feed" the needs of the group working with the data.

The data first used should be those associated with measurement of what the district has identified as its "key indicators" for success. It is easy to get lost in the morass of the "data swamp" if one does not use "key indicators" as a type of compass.

When starting out, start with small issues—small chunks of data—and practice the RCA process. Pick the low fruit first. Enable success by not attempting to tackle problems that have remained unsolvable for years.

Keep the process an open one. In other words, share your work with the whole staff, as appropriate, so that they can "verify" what has been developed to date. The following example demonstrates the need for such verification:

Example:

A region was having difficulty with enrollment in its distance learning courses. A large amount of resources had been allocated to the construction and development of fiber-optically-connected distance learning rooms in a dozen schools. A myriad of courses were being offered. Yet, enrollment after three years of programming remained low. At a closed meeting, the administrators charged with responsibility for the program listed what they saw as the primary causes for the low enrollment. These involved technical issues, personnel issues, and issues of scheduling both the courses and registration. Action plans were developed for each, and implementation began. A fishbone diagram was prepared and shared with all within the distance learning system who had not been part of the process. It quickly became apparent that the work group had missed the major point—the courses being offered did not fulfill the needs of the schools or the students. Upon further investigation, that opinion could be verified—yet it had totally escaped the combined wisdom of the group assigned to "find the problem."

The example above reminds us that as far as we have come in trying to develop representative work groups, it is impossible to have everyone around the table. We need, therefore, to bring the others on board through a "verification process" as the work is being worked upon. One planning facilitator said something to the effect that: "I can't share the plan, it isn't done yet." This completely misses the point. The plan must be shared if it is to be viable upon completion. It would be nice to think that even an isolated teacher working in the confines of her single classroom could find and be comfortable with checking her thinking with skilled and understanding colleagues.

Another way of keeping the process open is to include what Victoria Bernhardt refers to as "perceptive data." What do various groups think about this issue? Perceptive data can be gathered through a variety of means such as surveys, feedback forms, focus groups, and interviews.

Timing is also important. There should not only be adequate quality time to meet, think, and discuss, but time should also be arranged in such a way that the process does not drag out, yet still provides time for reflection and the consideration of new data and feedback from constituents. Spacing between meetings should not be so great as to interfere with continuity, nor should meetings be so close as not to allow time for the gathering and analysis of additional data. Meetings scheduled no sooner than every two weeks and no later than every three weeks work best in most instances.

As previously emphasized, the importance of committed leadership to the success of the root cause analysis process cannot be overstated.

Thus, although the specific setting and modality for a root cause analysis will vary, there are many supporting attributes that are the same. These are:

- Starting with data focused on key indicators of success
- Additional support for data gathering and analysis
- Starting with small, solvable issues
- Verification, openness and feedback
- Adequate time and timing
- Committed leadership

Change, Transformation, and RCA

Why use root cause analysis except to change? Most immediately, we want to change results, or to dissolve a problem. However, at a deeper level, the use of root cause analysis will also bring about changes in how we do the business of school.

While working with schools, one sometimes gains the sense that people in schools want to improve but that they do not want to change. They want to do what they have always done, but do it harder, better, or more efficiently. Root cause analysis can be used to that end, but it is like using a fine chisel to drive screws. Schools as they are presently structured and cultured, are doing a great job of accomplishing what they were originally structured to do. In order to improve results by any degree of magnitude, the structure and culture of schools has to change. Jim Leonard says it this way:

> The American education system is not broken; it's operating precisely
> as it was designed to operate; it's producing precisely what it was de-

signed to produce. The system's not broken; why reform it? Our schools do not need reform or restructuring. The American education system is in need of transformation and transformation implies a change of state. Organizations truly working on transformation no longer have the same priorities, the same concerns, the same problems. pp. 2–3

Root cause analysis is best used as part of a package of skills, knowledge, and beliefs that will enable fundamental change in how we approach schooling. The elements of the package include:

♦ Understanding systems

♦ Creating an open, collaborative culture

♦ Data-based decision making

♦ Accountability for results

♦ Distributed leadership

♦ Knowing what is important—key indicators

♦ Belief that all children can, and should, learn

Schools cannot be "transformed" without changing. Transformational change is deep change that occurs at the systems level. As Leonard stated, priorities, concerns, and problems will all change. Some other things that will change are:

♦ Role of administrators and teachers

♦ Role of students and parents

♦ Processes and systems within the school system

♦ The way the "business" of schooling is conducted

♦ How we think about things

Root cause analysis can be both a tool for finding cause, and when conducted properly, a medium for enabling systemic change. As a tool, RCA provides us with a series of concepts and processes that will lead us to deeper levels of causation. We can then act to dissolve the causes, rather than applying patches to the system. As a medium, RCA requires that we use, and therefore model, new modes of thinking, relating, acting, and structuring. These new roles, processes, and insights will enable, and indeed call for, acceleration of the transformation.

Bottom Line: at the building or district level, one cannot "buy into" just part of the package and be successful. Root cause analysis comes with a lot of necessary baggage that will bring about improvement, but also change. Know what (and why) you are starting, and commit to it, before you begin the journey.

In rereading the above section, doubts surfaced about the "severity" of the immediately preceding paragraph and the implications of Jim Leonard's call for transformation. There was an urge to soften words or to delete them entirely. The whole topic had been discarded only to be brought back. However, for honesty's sake, it was decided that these thoughts must be shared.

We educators are living in truly revolutionary times. Much of what Alvin Toffler predicted in *Future Shock* (1970) has come true, or is coming true. Here is what Toffler said in a recent interview:

> Our education system is a second-rate, factory-style organization pumping out obsolete information in obsolete ways. And it's not just that they haven't gotten the science books updated. They are simply not connected to the future of the kids they are responsible for. All education springs from some inner image of the future. It springs from some implicit assumptions about what the future holds. When your kid comes home and says, "Why do I need to learn Algebra?" you don't say, "Because our forefathers learned it." You tell them that you'll need it in the future. That assumes you know what the future has to hold. You'll need algebra, or you'll need marketing, or something. That presupposes that the parents and the curricula designers and the educators are making a set of assumptions about what the society, the colony of the world, is going to be like. If the model that you have in your head is of a smokestack, assembly-line economy, then you're preparing kids perfectly for that, as you've been doing for the past century or more. You're treating them like raw material. You're subjecting them to routine processing—totally de-individualized, mass-produced, without much care for the individual child. Moreover, you are giving the child repetitive work to do in preparation for a lifetime of repetitive work in the factories and factory-style offices that the kid is going to spend his life in. So for the past 100 to 150 years, we were more or less accurately sealing in the future of the kids.

> Now we're lying to the kids, because this process doesn't map onto what the kids are going to find when they get out the door. When I worked in the factory, if the boss knew I was reading a book on company time, I would be canned, instantaneously. I figured out a way to do my job faster and I could steal a couple of minutes to read. But he didn't want my head. He wanted my muscles. Now we are going to

want employees who are contractors or individuals working with us who innovate, imagine, think, challenge."

Toffler, Business2.com, September 26, 2000, pp. 115-116

Toffler's point is that drastic societal change has left the basic structure of school misaligned with the future. Each one of us has to decide if that is indeed reality. For those who agree, change must be seen as both necessary and inevitable.

Phillip Schechty, in his book, *Inventing Better Schools* shares the following thoughts:

> I have come to the conclusion that change is peculiarly difficult in schools because the schools, and the school districts of which they are typically a part, lack the capacities needed to support and sustain change efforts."
>
> If substantial, purposeful change is to occur and be sustained over time, the organization that is the subject of the change must possess three critical capacities:
>
> 1. The capacity to establish and maintain a focus on the future
>
> 2. The capacity to maintain a constant direction
>
> 3. The capacity to act strategically

School districts in Schelecty's "Standard Bearer Network" agree to work toward 10 standards that are at the heart of the school improvement process developed by his Center for Leadership in School Reform (CLSR). Standard One is:

> *Developing a Shared Understanding for the Need for Change*: The members of the Board of Education, the superintendent, central office staff, principals, teachers, leaders, leaders of parent organizations, and key community leaders have a common understanding of the nature of the problems and opportunities that confront the school district and base their discussions of these issues on a common body of fact and information." (data and root cause!!)

More time and space have been devoted to this thread than originally intended. Nevertheless, it is essential that RCA and all processes designed to enable student learning to improve must be placed in this broader context of school transformation, continuous school improvement, and systemic change.

The Obvious and Not So Obvious

Sometime ago, during a presentation by a member of the New York State Education Department, the comment was made that there are three types of problems:

1. Those for which we know the problem and the solution;

2. Those for which we know the problem but need to find a solution; and

3. Those for which we know neither the problem nor the solution.

The speaker indicated that much of what we deal with in schools is in the third category. For school leaders, the trick has become knowing, for sure, which of the three types of problems we are dealing with. Sometimes, we think we know what the "problem" is when, in fact, we are acting on beliefs, opinions, stereotypes, hunches, etc. We then jump quickly to the solution phase and typically, once again, apply strategies that have not worked before—only we do them harder, in a more focused way, etc.

A similar set of thoughts came to mind as I was working with a large Midwestern urban school system. I was called in to do some training, rather than facilitation. In discussions with some of the top leadership, who are also very proactive in focusing on results, I again came to realize that many times both the problem and the solution are obvious. If, for example, one observes a class or building that is in utter chaos with no evidence of effective leadership, one must move quickly to bring the situation into control without a prolonged exercise searching for root cause. Once control is established, however, I would want to sit down and study the various factors that led up to the incident, e.g., by asking whether there were problems in training, in hiring, in supervision, etc. Thus, even if I must quickly put out a fire, I will do so, but then will reflect on why the fire started in the first place. The question becomes: can we avoid such an incident in the future?

Using a mechanical metaphor—which is not always perfect—a car once stopped as if it ran out of gas. It was towed to a garage where the mechanic saw that the gas filter was completely clogged. The immediate solution was a new gas filter. The driver quickly went on his way, only to have the car come to a halt just three blocks from the service station. When it was examined yet again, it was found that the gas filter was again completely blocked. The next identified "cause" was sand that had been placed in the gas tank. Once the tank was removed and cleaned, the problem did not happen again. If the driver had wanted to avoid a similar occurrence, he could have purchased a lockable gas cap.

What's the point? It is that in some instances we can indeed make an immediate and correct professional diagnosis and "solve" a problem. It is difficult to quantify what percentage of problems fall into this range. However, observing the folks out in the Midwest, a certain level of confidence developed that they were making accurate diagnosis of what, perhaps, were obvious problems with obvious solutions. On the other hand, one must retain a certain level of caution because what appears to be obvious, such as the clogged gas filter, may not necessarily be the primary cause.

Once upon a time in a secondary school, it seemed that vandalism and general negative behavior on the part of students was on the rise. Faculty generally ascribed the problem to the lack of discipline, and, in their view, consequences for students were not sufficiently severe. The faculty called for an immediate crackdown on offenders. Another point of view looked at what was happening within the school. A wide range of students was not being successful. Over half of all students failed courses. Nearly half of all students were not participants in any area of school life other than classes. Extracurricular activities were focused on the academic, and sports teams were dominated by the "preps." A third area of potential cause could be found in the understandings (or lack of them) that faculty and administration had regarding their respective responsibility for student behavior and building climate. Could all three "root cause" areas have been operational? Perhaps so. But without a deeper analysis of the perceived "problem," any steps taken would not have been helpful except by chance—and, indeed, some of them could have been downright counterproductive.

This is not real simple stuff. Yet, on the other hand, it should not be treated as a mystical process. We just need to get away from the tradition of "knee-jerk" response to problems using a catalog of tired solutions—many of which are patches. Not only is the search for root cause a tool to dissolving the problem, it is a generative process that changes the level of discussion and refocuses the participants on deeper underlying issues, such as organizational culture, which have often been ignored. In many ways, the process of searching is as beneficial as the find.

A Timetable for Meetings

The model below is based upon the process of questioning data explained in Chapter 3. It will vary somewhat if other processes are used, and may vary depending on the difficulty of the issue being explored.

Prior to the First Meeting

Issue a Level One data set(s) to members of the group that will be conducting the analysis. The data should be measurement(s) of a key indicator or indicators. This may be a district team, committee, department, or whole faculty. Allow them several days to review the data with two questions in mind:

1. What do I see in the data?

2. What questions do I have about what I see.

First Meeting—2 Hours

Divide the group into smaller groups of 3 to 6, depending upon the overall size of the group. Individuals are to share within their smaller group what they have seen in the data. Each smaller group then discusses the items with the intent of identifying a maximum of six priority issues that they want to share with the total group. These should be red-flag issues. Each group then reports out. Typically, the first groups have more to share than later groups because the later groups find that "their" red-flag issues have already been shared. When all red-flag issues have been identified, they should be paretoed as to which are the most immediate and more important. This is a process of assigning each item a priority weight. (I use a simple 1-3-5 system, with 1 being the lowest priority and five being the highest.) Once they have been prioritized in this manner, take the top 3 to 6 items and ask each smaller group to reconvene to list what questions they have about these issues. Repeat the reporting out process above. The products from this session include:

♦ a complete listing of what was seen

♦ a prioritized listing of most immediate items

♦ a series of questions that need to be answered for each of the most immediate (prioritized) items

♦ data gathering to be completed prior to the next meeting

Between the First and Second Meeting—1 to 3 Weeks

Insofar as possible, the data necessary to answer the questions raised at the first meeting should be gathered and distributed to the members of the larger group. This should be a rule of thumb for all meetings—get the data into their hands at least a day or two before the next meeting. Ask members to review the data for what they see and to form questions before they arrive at the meeting. Do not waste precious meeting time going over data that folks have never seen before. This process requires central-office support in terms of clerical and administrative time to track down the data and place it into a presentable form.

Sometimes, the data needs to be developed, via survey, feedback forms, or other means. This will sometimes take a long time. If that is the case, especially with some essential information, the group can move on to another issue, returning to the preceding issue when the data is available.

Example:

A school district had a specific interest in the level of engagement students had with their school. In brief, the committee made the decision to survey students, using a nationwide instrument which had a substantial research base and history of use. However, the survey was objected to by parents in a nearby state, which caused the local school district to turn the process over to attorneys to make sure it was done in a satisfactory manner. This delayed the gathering of data for approximately six months. The issue, however, was never out of sight, and the committee was able to process other priority issues in the interim.

At the Second Meeting—2 Hours

Quickly review the new data, and clarify anything that needs clarification. Repeat the questioning data process—what is seen in these new data sets? What questions do we have about these new items we see? Now we can begin to ask the group about its hunches about what appears to be some causal areas. Here is where professional knowledge and experience, as informed by the data, can be added without great fear of simply resorting to opinion. The products from this session again include:

♦ a complete listing of what was seen in the new data

♦ a prioritized listing of most immediate items

♦ a series of questions that need to be answered for each of the most immediate items

♦ data gathering to be completed prior to the next meeting

Between the Second and Third Meeting

Additional data gathering has to be conducted. However it is time to share the products to date with the whole staff and ask for their feedback. They should be told of the data sets examined, the issues selected as priorities, the follow-up data being used, and the hunches that have been laid out on the table. They should then be asked to respond with ideas of their own for the committee to consider at its next meeting. Any new data and the feedback from the full staff should be shared with the committee a few days prior to the next meeting.

Many formal and informal channels of communication are operative between meetings. This helps provide information and feedback coming to and going from members of the committee. Often, administration will convene meetings with special groups that are associated with the issue. The whole system can easily be engaged with proper leadership and understanding of the process.

At the Third Meeting—2 Hours

At this point, the committee may very well be close to being smothered in data. The point is to emerge with some specific causes or causal areas. How this is accomplished will be up to the facilitator. It is usually worked through a variety of smaller group/larger group discussions and various forms of paretoing. At the end of the session, however, the group should emerge with a good deal of confidence that it has located significant causes that need to be addressed. Members should be asked to think of various strategies between now and the fourth meeting.

Between the Third and Fourth Meetings

Again, the product from the third meeting should be shared with the total staff. These are the significant causes or causal areas that are being focused upon.

The Fourth Meeting—2 Hours

Feedback from staff is dealt with, and it is at this meeting that specific strategies are identified and action plans developed for their implementation. If the selection of strategies is beyond the knowledge and skill base of the committee, it is perfectly proper for the committee to "delegate" this task to a more appropriate group while maintaining control over the process. If, for example, the strategies must be in the area of early literacy, and the committee does not have the necessary expertise in this area, the topic may be turned over to a committee formed for this special purpose or to an existing curriculum committee. If so, the fourth meeting would be devoted to a report of this group and a discussion to confirm the strategies and action plan.

If the time between meetings is kept to 2 to 3 weeks, this entire process can be accomplished anywhere between six and nine weeks. As indicated above, however, the gathering of some necessary data may extend the process. Likewise, some simpler issues may be accomplished in a much shorter period of time. The length of time will also vary depending upon where in the organization the root cause analysis is taking place (classroom, department/program, building, or whole district) and the modality being used (positive/negative—reactive/proactive). With a reasonable understanding of the process and its features, most all will be able to easily tailor a root cause analysis to their specific setting and needs.

Using Gantt Charts

A modified Gantt Chart has been presented in Figures 5.1 and 5.2 to illustrate another scenario involving root cause analysis—a K–8 district mathematics committee seeking cause for lower-than-desired student math proficiency as measured by state assessments. Gantt Charts are useful for communicating process plans to all stakeholders and for monitoring implementation and completion of each step.

Figure 5.1. Modified Gantt Chart—Page One: First Year

What	Who	Year One July	Aug	Sept	Oct	Nov	Dec	Jan	Feb	Mar	April	May	June	Year Two July	Aug
Review Math 4 & 8 assessment data using diagnostic tree Identify preliminary causal areas. Benchmark	The K-8 Math Committee	▓												▓	▓
Analyze assessment results including item analysis	Faculty Math Assessment Subcommittee	▓												▓	▓
Report findings to full staff for verification/ Feedback	The K-8 Math Committee and/or Assessment Subcommittee		▓		▓		→	▓							
Integrate feedback and continue RCA in depth. Benchmark	The K-8 Math Committee		▓	▓	▓			▓							
Identify Fundamental Root Causes and Immediate and Longer Term Strategies for Improvement	The K-8 Math						▓								
Implement Immediate Strategies	Principal Faculty Committee				▓	▓	▓	▓					▓		
Plan & budget for implementation of Longer-Term Strategies	Principal Faculty Committee				▓	▓	▓	▓					▓		
Monitor process	The K-8 Math Committee	▓	▓	▓	▓	▓	▓	▓	▓	▓	▓	▓	▓	▓	▓

Key Indicator: Student proficiency in mathematics as measured by state assessments.

Desired Ideal Condition: 100% of all students achieve proficiency by the completion of 8th grade.

Present Condition: Over the last three years the percentage of proficiency at the end of 8th grade was, respectively, 62%, 59%, and 65%.

Goal Statement: Over the course of the next three years, we will improve the level of student proficiency to 100% by the end of the 8th grade (75%, 85%, 100%).

Figure 5.2. Modified Gantt Chart—Page Two: Second Year

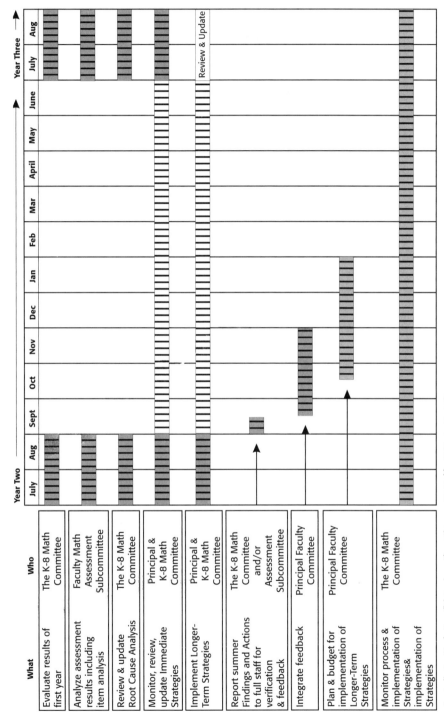

Key Indicator: Student proficiency in mathematics as measured by state assessments.
Desired Ideal Condition: 100% of all students achieve proficiency by the completion of 8th grade.
Present Condition: Over the last three years, the percentage of proficiency at the end of 8th grade was respectively, 62%, 59%, and 65%.
Goal Statement: Over the course of the next three years, we will improve the level of student proficiency to 100% by the end of the 8th grade (75%, 85%, 100%).

The first two columns provide information regarding what is to be done and who is responsible. In this case, responsibilities rest with committees or the principal. In other cases, specific people may be named. The more specifically one can identify both "what" and "who," the more useful this tool becomes.

Note that this chart also contains information regarding the key indicator, desired ideal condition, present condition, and goal statement. These must be kept visible and current as constant reminders of purpose and need.

The next 14 columns cover a period of 14 months and provide space for the extension of timelines for each step of the process. In this example, considerable initial work is conducted over the summer months in preparation for reporting back to full staff for verification and feedback soon after school opens in September. Continuing reporting back occurs in the second half of October, and again during the beginning of January. Initial feedback is used by the committee to conduct deeper root cause analysis and benchmarking during September and October, with final identification of fundamental root causes and strategies to be completed by January first.

Although this six-month period may appear to be longer than necessary, it takes time to gather and analyze all the data necessary to eliminate or confirm root cause hypotheses and to adequately benchmark with more successful school districts. If curriculum misalignment is suspected, curriculum mapping can take a semester or more, or it may be delayed until summer. Selection of appropriate strategies also requires research of the literature and benchmarking to identify best practice.

As indicated earlier in this chapter, some root causes may be confirmed early on in the process as obvious. Identification, implementation, planning, and budgeting for strategies to dissolve these roots can begin as soon as agreement on their identity is reached. Hence, the bar representing implementation, planning, and budgeting begins soon after the initial report to staff, but continues on as less obvious and deeper roots are exposed as.

Page two of the chart presents activities for the second year, and even for the summer of the third year. For problems of this size and scope, it is important that RCA become an intentional, sustained, and dynamic process focused on solving the issue at hand.

Gantt Charts can also be used to communicate implementation of each specific strategy, such as staff development, curriculum alignment, the selection of a new textbook series, a plan to retain and mentor new staff, changes in scheduling or grouping, or development of student support programs.

The Team Charter

The sample team charter below was written specifically for work in New York State with Comprehensive District Education Planning (CDEP) teams. The point of "team," however, is valid whether one is talking about a district or building planning team, or if one is discussing a team formed for the process of root cause analysis. The concept of "team" and knowing what one's purpose and mode of operation is, remain the same no matter what state one is in or what process is used. Throughout this text, various terms have been used to describe the collection of individuals responsible for school improvement or root cause analysis efforts. They have been variously identified as "groups," "committees," or "teams." Because it has been found that teams, and prior experience with teaming, have positive impact on the quality of outcomes from school improvement processes such as CDEP, it is evident that movement from "committee thinking" to "team thinking" is beneficial.

Successful committees may be composed of relatively independent individuals. A true team, on the other hand, has a shared commitment to its vision and task that creates both synergy and energy greater than the sum of the individual parts. Teams are interdependent with many linkages and connections. Teams are much more collaborative than committees. Individuals within teams must trust and remove boundaries that separate. Team members create and share a common team culture and bond.

Moving a committee toward being a team requires understanding, training, and sustained commitment on the part of all involved. Larry Lozette[1] is reported as identifying the five reasons listed for team failure:

1. Members don't understand the team mission.

2. Members don't understand their own roles or responsibilities.

3. Members don't understand how to do their task or how to work as part of the team.

4. Members don't buy into the team's function, purpose or goals.

5. Members reject their roles and responsibilities.

Sue Tucker[2] amplifies Lozette's observations with the following comments:

---

1 Work Teams in Schools (ERIC Document Reproduction Services No. ED391226)
2 Tucker, S. (1995). *Benchmarking: A Guide for Educators*, p. 29. Corwin Press.

A team works best when everyone involved understands its purpose and goals. The most frequent problems that teams encounter include the following:

- Lack of agreement on the purpose of the work

- Switches in direction

- Lack of common definitions of success for the team's work

- Feelings held by members that the project is too big or inappropriate

- Excessive questioning of each decision

- Lack of knowledge or resources to deal with the issue

Most planning failures and team problems can be traced to confusion about the purpose, expected outcomes, authority, resources, or timelines of the team. Take as much time as necessary to clarify these issues up front, among and between the team members and administration.

Why Write a Team Charter?

A team charter is a tool that can be used to minimize the negative forces identified by Lozette and Tucker.

Figure 5.3. A Sample Team Charter

Team Name:	The Comprehensive District Education Plan Team (CDEP Team)
Charge:	To identify and improve specific areas of student achievement through the use of CDEP.
Operational Values:	♦ Systems Thinking
	♦ Data-based inquiry and decision making
	♦ Seeking root cause
	♦ Focus on student results first, rather than on means
	♦ Continuous improvement
	♦ Inclusion and involvement of all stakeholders
	♦ Sharing and distribution of tasks
	♦ Honesty
Authority:	♦ Constituted and supported by the Superintendent of Schools, with the knowledge, and backing of the Board of Education, to complete its charge.

♦ The CDEP team reports to the Superintendent of Schools or his/her designee.

Responsibility:

♦ To learn and complete the CDEP process to the very best of its ability.

♦ To identify specific priority areas of "need" based upon data.

♦ To seek root cause for each problem.

♦ To identify strategies to dissolve the causes in order to improve learning.

♦ To develop an action plan for each strategy.

♦ To evaluate both implementation and results.

♦ To involve and inform all stakeholder groups.

♦ To submit preliminary findings to verification process prior to finalization.

♦ To submit the CDEP to the Superintendent of Schools in a timely fashion.

Resources:

♦ CDEP and team training/facilitation.

♦ Data preparation and analysis.

♦ School clerical services.

♦ Other district teams and committees as needed.

♦ Meeting room (space).

♦ Planning notebooks.

♦ Access to information.

♦ Budget information and access.

♦ School in-house CDEP coordinator.

♦ Meeting times and materials for an eight-month period.

Appointment: Team members are appointed by the Superintendent of Schools for one annual planning cycle and may be reappointed for continuing terms.

Decisions: Team decisions will be by consensus rather than vote. Any individual who strongly opposes a decision will be heard by the team. However, complete unanimity will not be required.

Timeline:

♦ Based upon year-end data—the planning team will commence its work in July and continue until February 1 when its final plan will be submitted to the Superintendent of Schools for approval by the Board of Education at its February meeting. This will enable its recommendations to fit into the budget, staff development, and staffing schedules while making use of the latest data on student achievement.

♦ Meetings will be scheduled no less frequently than biweekly and will be scheduled in such a manner as to permit participation of all team members over time. No meetings will extend beyond three hours except by approval of the team.

Functioning: The team may from time to time separate into smaller task forces or work groups in order to accomplish specific tasks. The team may delegate specific tasks to other teams or groups within the school, asking them to report back to the CDEP Team as a whole. The team will be facilitated through the CDEP process, and the school district will provide an internal leader or coordinator in support of the logistics of the process.

End Products: A completed Comprehensive District Educational Plan including:

♦ Identification of key "red flag" issues supported by data

♦ Identification of root causes for each

♦ Identification of strategies to dissolve the root causes

♦ A complete action plan for each strategy

♦ A means of monitoring and evaluating progress of each action plan and changes in student results

♦ Support items:
  • District statement—outlining its present context
  • Areas of success
  • Listing of committee members and groups represented

Foundations—Systems, Data, and Variation

Root cause analysis is a process that is most productive when embedded in a rich context of supporting knowledge, skills, and concepts. The purpose the following final topics is to briefly review three areas that are necessary foundations for sound root cause analysis.

1. Systems Thinking

2. Data

3. Variation and Statistical Process Control

It is essential that school leaders understand and grasp the significance of each of these topics before going too far down the road in using root cause problem-solving processes.

Systems Thinking

Jim Leonard (1996) states that "systems thinking assigns most differences in student performance to the system—not to the student." W. Edwards Deming

(1982) states that: "apparent differences between people arise almost entirely from action of the system they work in, not from the people themselves." Root cause analysis, then, is not employed to place blame, but rather to determine those components of the system that need to be improved. It is a systems-focused, rather than people-focused, process.

Administrators often complain about tenured staff who are not producing desired results. This may very well be. However, who recruited that person? Who hired that person? Who supervised, mentored, and oriented that person, and who recommended that person for tenure? What staff development was employed to strengthen that person? What is the climate and culture of the work place in which that person is employed? The questions could go on, but the point is made. System variables far outnumber the single entity of the dysfunctional staff member.

The ability of a person to perform is a function, not only of the person's abilities, but also of that person's supporting system. In the case of a teacher, it involves all that was mentioned above plus things such as materials, methods, facilities, degree of collegial support, time, and a host of other system inputs. In the case of a student, the system of support can include: home setting, parental support, ability of the teacher, instructional materials, supplies and setting. Jim Leonard correctly points out that when we "grade" a student we are in fact grading the whole of the student's system of support—not just the effort, ability, or achievement of the student. This is a key point. Without understanding that we are seeking cause, rather than blame, the whole process will be for naught. As Leonard states:

> Significant breakthroughs in the quality of learning in our schools will come only from addressing all major sources of variation in the process—not the student (or teacher) alone.

Russell Ackoff on Systems

In November, 1993, I attended one of the Goal/QPC conferences in Boston. Never underestimate the power of such conferences. In this case, it was a single phrase uttered by Russell Ackoff that changed my thinking forever. Ackoff was presenting to a large group on systems thinking and said:

> A system is not the sum of its parts, but rather, the product of the interaction of the parts.

It was as if a thousand light bulbs went off in my head all at once. For years I had focused on the improvement of parts—now I was being told that the key was in the interaction of the parts—the white space between the parts. For me it was both revelation and transformation. I have not seen the world the same since. Once one jumps "over the broom" into the world of systems thinking, one can never go back. As an educator, I looked at schools differently—seeing how the lack of proper interactions among the parts blocked the success of the system as a whole. I saw clearly for the first time the magnitude of how fragmented schools really are. We have built walls between programs, grade levels, buildings, subject areas, departments, and funding sources. We create numerous, isolated plans focused on segments of the whole. As a consumer, I cannot help but see the mark of system interactions, or their absence, when I purchase an item in a store, eat at a restaurant, or act as a customer in hundreds of other situations.

I need to share the rest of what Russell Ackoff shared at that conference:

> A system consists of a set of parts—each part effects all parts; no part has an independent effect on the whole; if you put parts together into subsets—each subset effects all subsets and no one subset has an independent effect on the whole.

The meaning for me, and for those working to improve schools, is that within a system, everything is connected. You cannot change one part without impacting the whole system. Although a high school staff seeking to solve a learning issue may have some success, it is only when the whole system leading up to high school is also engaged in the process that large scale success is possible.

Continuing this same train of thought on the qualities of a system, Ackoff went on:

> The system is a whole which can not be divided into independent parts.

> When a system is taken apart it loses its essential properties.

> If you focus on optimization of parts you will not improve the system.

> Performance of the system depends on how the parts fit—not on how good the parts are.

And finally! Once again!

> Systems are not the sum of their parts—they are the product of their interactions.

On my desk, I have a clear plastic box containing a disassembled wristwatch. It is my attempt at making Ackoff's statements both concrete and visible. The sum of the parts in the box are equal to the sum of the parts in the watch on my wrist, yet, the parts in the box do not tell me the time, date, day of the week, or any other information that the watch on my wrist continues to provide. I can attempt to improve the parts in the box, piece by piece, but that will not improve the functioning of the parts in the plastic box. Only when they are once again properly linked can they interact in such a way as to perform the functions of a watch. As separate parts, they have lost their essential nature. They are no longer a watch—just parts in a box.

The metaphor of the watch parts is a strong one for me as I look at the fragmentation within our schools. Most schools remain a collection of parts. It is a wonder that they perform at all. No doubt there must be some connections and interactions taking place. But, to improve schools requires a much deeper look at how we have isolated the parts within the system. I have no doubt that many of the root causes we are seeking are found at the level of inadequate interactions.

Here are some parting words from Russell Ackoff:

> The problems of education are not out there in society or the culture—they are in the heads of the people in this room (mostly educators)—and we have to break out of our own self-imposed constraints.

> Effective management of organized behavior is management of interactions, not actions. The deficiencies in the educational system cannot be removed by changing only the content of education…The message its structures and processes deliver are more seriously misleading and counterproductive than any messages delivered in courses.

What Is Systems Thinking?—A Summary

When working with school districts on the concept of systems, use the following ideas to present the concept of systems:[3]

- ◆ Systems thinking is an approach to organizational improvement based on awareness of the whole, the part, and the interactions between the two.

- ◆ Systems thinking focuses on root causes for problems (not symptoms or blame), the behaviors flowing from assumptions and beliefs, and the structures shaped by them.

- ◆ Organizational outcomes are the end result of a complex equation. Changes in that outcome can only come from a thorough understanding of and adjustment to the whole equation.

- ◆ The output of a system is primarily influenced by processes rather than by individuals.

---

3 This section is based on an adaptation and expansion of ideas expressed in Asayesh, G. (1993, Fall). Using systems thinking to change systems. *Journal of Staff Development*, 14(4) 8–12.

- Systems thinking is understanding the connections between people and processes in organizations so that we can continuously improve our work.

- Systems thinking is about seeing the whole.

- Systems thinking is the only way to achieve long-term improvement.

- Systems thinkers believe structure influences behavior.

Systems thinking requires:

- Extensive staff development in understanding, and the belief in, the knowledge and tools of system thinking.

- Collaboration among individuals representing a cross-section of a school system.

- Changing the way we think and discarding traditional assumptions.

- Long-term thinking.

- Initial pain.

What can we do?

- Become a systems thinker.

- Learn the concepts and adopt the beliefs.

- Use the tools.

- Teach our students system thinking. Use the class, the building, and the program as our system.

- Don't work on committees that do not use systems thinking—it is a waste of time and is dishonest.

There is so much more to learn about systems, but this is not a guide about systems, and this information should be sufficient to lay the necessary groundwork of understandings necessary for successful root cause analysis. The Bibliography in Chapter 7 contains many texts that amplify and dig more deeply into the concept of systems thinking.

Data

One of the most consistent issues schools run into while trying to conduct root cause analysis is their inability to easily organize and successfully use data. It seems that although schools are awash in a plethora of data, they find data to be a very scarce commodity in useable form.

School data are often stored in many different formats, few, if any of which, are compatible. Data can be found on paper, cards, microfilm, and a wide variety of computer programs. Their location can also be widely distributed across the district, as are the people responsible as "data owners." The problem of accuracy has also reared its ugly head in a variety of processes. It appears that for years, data was not taken seriously and, hence, the correctness of data was not a concern.

The one exception to this state of affairs is in the area of "data with a $." In the case of money, it appears, we have a small army to account for every penny. Did you ever try to get reimbursed for a legitimate expense without having a receipt? Stories can be told of large amounts of time spent over issues of 18 or 14 cents. "Data with a $" has to be audited, by law in New York State, each year, and the outside auditor's report has to be publicly presented at a meeting of the Board of Education of each school district. But what about data concerning our primary responsibility—learning? It typically sits in boxes, unwanted and unused. With the advent of the accountability and standards movement, however, this is rapidly changing. The No Child Left Behind legislation will ensure the rapid development of data warehousing capacity. Within the last three years, significant numbers of school systems are moving to data warehousing, retrieval, and querying systems that would have been unthinkable just a short time ago. Soon, we will have more than sufficient data, in correct and workable form, to conduct the most sophisticated of root cause analysis procedures. For the present, however, schools without adequate data capacity must be content to begin the process with the data on hand. Hopefully, all schools are coming to realize that data about learning is at least as equally important as data about dollars.

What Kinds of Data?

Schlecty (1997) indicates the kinds of data needed:

> System performance cannot, however, be assessed with single measures or even with multiple measures of single things. What is needed are multiple measures of multiple things, because systems are complex and understanding system performance means understanding this complexity." (p. 140)

Schlecty (1997) goes on (pp. 188–189) to identify five kinds of measures (data): They are:

1. Measures of results—test scores, teacher grades, absentee rates

2. Quality-control measures—level of student engagement

3. Process measures—product focus, novelty, authenticity of instruction

4. System performance measures—kinds of technology used, adequacy of staff skills, spatial requirements

5. Measures to describe and analyze properties of the system itself—rules, roles, relationships, culture, coordination, and status

Victoria Bernhardt approaches the same issue, but arrives at a different structure for the organization of data. She calls her model "multiple measures" and it divides data into four dimensions that, when combined, "allows the prediction of actions/processes/programs that best meet the needs of all students" (Data Analysis, p. 15). Dr. Bernhardt's four multiple measures are:

1. *Demographics*—enrollment, attendance, dropout rate, ethnicity, gender, language, and grade level

2. *Perceptions*—perceptions of learning environment, values and beliefs, attitudes, and observations

3. *Student Learning*—test scores and teacher observations

4. *School Processes*—description of school programs and processes

Edie Holcomb approaches the process in a slightly different way by asking five questions about data. They are:

1. What evidence would demonstrate that we are fulfilling the commitments embedded in our mission statement?

2. Do we have any existing, ongoing goals that lack baseline data from which to measure progress?

3. Is there more than one source of evidence for this decision or more than one indicator of need for this goal?

4. What are the assumptions we make about students and their learning, and what do we need to do to verify them?

5. What data might help resolve smoldering issues in our school?

The North-Central Association of Colleges and Schools requires schools to develop a profile based on the following (adapted from Holcomb):

♦ Unique local insights

♦ Follow-up of former students

♦ Data on student characteristics

♦ Instructional data

♦ Community data

We could go on, but the point is made that there is both a wide variety of different types of data and numerous ways to structure or organize the collection of those data. Dr. Bernhardt's concept of multiple measures of data has proven to be easily used in clarifying the concept of using multiple data sources and types when working with school districts teams.

There are also at least two ways to approach the study of data. The first is to scan all data—looking for red-flag issues—and then seek to solve the problems indicated by the red flags. The second is to concentrate the scanning of data only on measures of key indicators of school and student success. The second approach is better for the following reasons listed:

♦ By scanning all data, it is easy for a group to get "lost" in a morass of insignificant details.

♦ Although red flags may be identified, there is no guarantee that the red flags are the important issues associated with key indicators.

♦ Typically, scanning all data results in scanning only the data that are readily available rather than data associated with key indicators.

On the other hand, if one begins with the key indicators, these issues are minimized. Here is a possible sequence of initial data activities, beginning with the key indicators:

♦ Identify and select your key indicators of student success.

♦ Select several measures for each key indicator keeping in mind the variety of data "available."

♦ Gather the data for each of the several measures for each key indicator.

♦ Scan all data sets for red flags.

♦ Confirm the red flags and begin the analysis of root cause through the use of one of the processes outlined in Chapter 3.

Levels of Data

For purposes of clarity, data can be identified as either "Level One" data or "Level Two" and beyond. Level One data is typically an initial aggregated data set prior to disaggregation or further analysis. An example may be a school's fourth-grade reading assessment results. Level One data is typically the starting point, and is most helpful in identification of major red-flag issues. "Level Two" data, and beyond, is a deeper data set—usually Level One data that has been disaggregated and analyzed further. Warning: it is sometimes possible that Level One data reveals no red flags, but that when the same data set is disaggregated, certain problems may appear—such as inequality among various student groups. Again, an important aspect of scanning data is to be able to "see" what it is telling and to ask pertinent questions of it for further analysis.

Transforming Data

Single pieces of data are not typically useful in and of themselves. Data must be transformed into information, knowledge, understanding, and wisdom. Hopefully, decisions are made on the basis of understanding and wisdom, rather than just at the data or information stages. This transformation takes place through the use of multiple measures, data analysis, benchmarking, discussion, and root cause analysis processes.

Although data warehousing and querying tools are very helpful in data analysis, much can also be accomplished with simple spreadsheet programs, such as Excel, or programs such as SPSS (Statistical Package for the Social Sciences). Again, the back room gathering, preparation, and initial analysis of data should be completed prior to team meetings by staff allocated for that purpose. The more important function for the team is in the interpretation of the data analysis and making decisions based on that interpretation.

Squishy Data Warning

Because of sample size, lack of data over time, and a myriad of other factors, school data are often soft, and, therefore, cannot withstand the rigors of significant statistical analysis. These data are said to be "squishy." At least seven points of data are needed to determine if true change has taken place or if it is just normal variation. In education, we rarely have seven points of data. The smaller the sample size, the greater the problem of variation. Often, schools do not have sufficient numbers within a cohort to be able to use data with a great deal of certainty. State assessments are new, and, frequently, only two or three data points are available for analysis. All of this contributes to the concept of "squishy data." Despite these causes for concern, school data can be used as a general measure to identify areas of weakness and to monitor progress toward goals. One just has to be aware of the limitations of school data and the pitfalls if they are used beyond their ability to statistically define.

Variation

All systems vary. *ALL SYSTEMS VARY!* Therefore, there will be variation in all of the data about your system. In order to better understand your system, you need to be able to understand its variation over time.

There are two types of variation—(a) common cause variation and (b) special cause variation.

Common cause variation is the variation that takes place within a system or process that is a normal part of the system or process. An illustration:

> A teacher drives eight miles from her house to her school, and can predict with reasonable certainty how long it will take to get to work, or, in the evening, to drive home. Driving to work and back home are both processes. Remember—all work is a process. Although she can predict that it will take between 12 and 16 minutes each way—she cannot predict each trip down to the second because of the normal, or common cause, variations that occur as part of the process. Common variations include such things as: making it through traffic lights or not, variable speed at which she drives—some days are slower than others—or getting behind a slow driver. Each of these causes is frequent enough that they become part of the common causes of variation in her driving time.

Special cause variation is caused by some type of special event or circumstance that is typically outside of the normal process. Let's continue with the illustration:

> One day, it took the teacher over half an hour to make the trip. This was way beyond the normal range of variation. The special cause was an accident that caused not only a delay but a rerouting that required her to turn around and find another way to her school. Other special causes could include a flat tire, engine failure, getting a ticket etc.

When a team looks at school data, it is essential to recognize that data will normally vary, and then it is important to be able to determine if the variation is being caused by common cause variation or if it is being caused by special causes. If it is mostly special cause, then the system is said to be out of control. Special cause variation needs to be eliminated before the system can be improved.

Going back to the driving example, if a flat tire occurs every day, or if one day there is a flat tire, the next day a ticket, the next day engine failure, and the next day the car runs out of gas—it might be said that the driving-to-work system is out of control. Before the basics of the system can be improved, we must be able to eliminate all of the special causes. Once they are gone, we can begin to work on the system, narrowing and improving the range of time that it takes to get to work. We can improve the system by studying the route. Perhaps another route will provide a reduced driving time to the school. Perhaps leaving a few minutes later or earlier will result in avoiding heavier traffic. Perhaps by attending to speed, making sure that it is always at maximum, a shorter trip can be assured. If travel time is a really important issue, moving closer to the job or finding a job closer to home should be considered. All of these are attempts at both narrowing the range of driving time and reducing it—within a system that is basically "in control."

There are tools that teams can use to determine if their system is in control. The control chart is a primary tool for determining if a system is "in control," and understanding how it operates will enable school leaders to make use of it to determine what is, and is not, normal variation in their data. Don Wheeler's text is a good detailed source on the use of control charts, as is *The Memory Jogger*. Both are listed in the Bibliography in Chapter 7.

Perhaps the best way to illustrate the concept of systems variation is to provide a specific example. The concept of systems variation is illustrated in Figure 5.4. The data table in Figure 5.4 contains New York State 11th-Grade English Regents data from 12 school districts within a single BOCES region. For purposes of this analysis, the 12 high schools are being treated as if they were all within one school district. The table shows the percentage of students in each high school who passed the regents exam. Schools are numbered in the far left column.

Figure 5.4. Data Table: New York State Comprehensive English Regents—Percent Passing

School	93-94	94-95	95-96	96-97	97-98	98-99	Average	Range
1	57	26	35	68	56	53	49	42
2	40	53	36	68	75	55	54	39
3	57	58	63	40	44	91	59	51
4	34	58	51	61	76	88	61	54
5	42	51	79	73	55	74	62	37
6	46	60	65	47	76	86	63	40
7	71	58	66	64	72	78	68	20
8	70	77	68	80	81	50	71	30
9	67	67	74	75	73	77	72	10
10	68	78	66	61	100	90	77	39
11	83	69	58	80	86	84	77	26
12	87	83	71	99	74	79	82	28
Average	60	65	63	68	74	77	68	17
Range	53	57	44	59	66	36	33	

Perhaps we need nothing more than the table in Figure 5.4 to understand how systems will vary. However, which is common cause and which is special cause variation? Let's see what we can find out.

When these data are plotted on a graph, they appear as seen in Figure 5.5 (page 156). The 12 school districts are arrayed along the X Axis, whereas the percentage of passing students is arrayed along the Y Axis. Six years of testing are indicated.

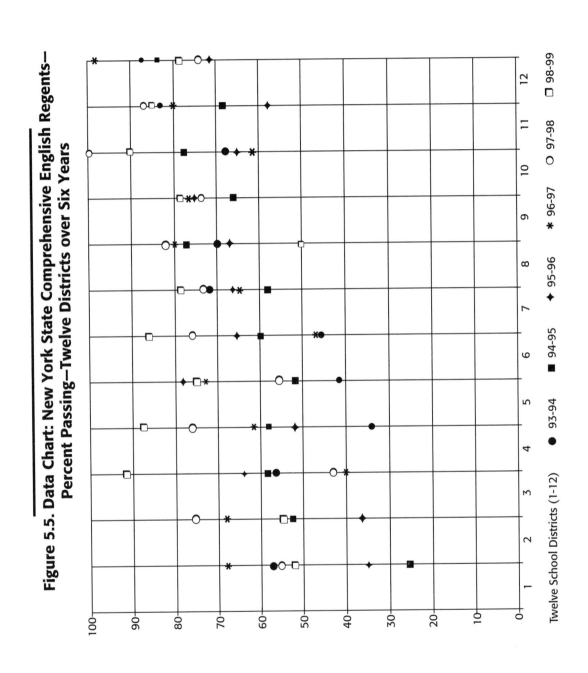

Figure 5.5. Data Chart: New York State Comprehensive English Regents—
Percent Passing—Twelve Districts over Six Years

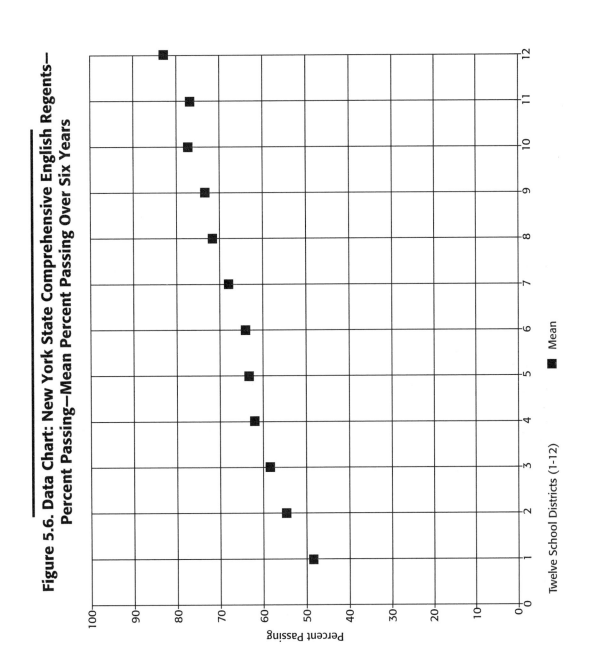

Figure 5.6. Data Chart: New York State Comprehensive English Regents—
Percent Passing—Mean Percent Passing Over Six Years

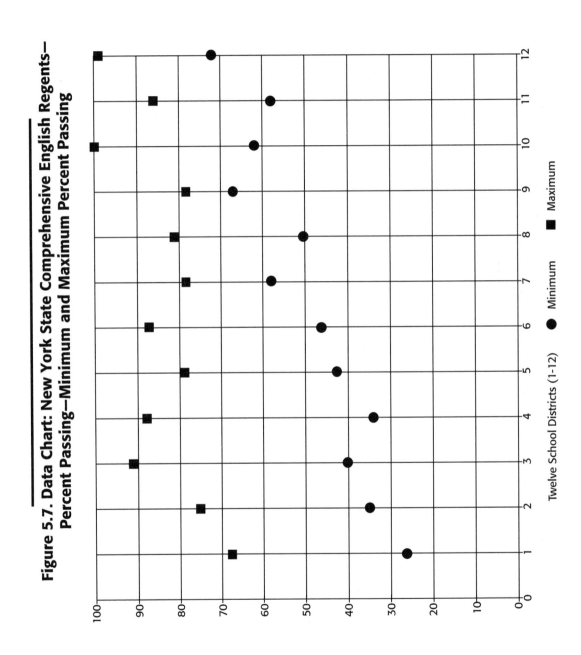

Figure 5.7. Data Chart: New York State Comprehensive English Regents—Percent Passing—Minimum and Maximum Percent Passing

It is obvious that some high schools are performing at a level that is higher than some others. Figure 5.6 (page 157) shows that the mean percent of passing students varies in a linear fashion from 49 percent in school 1 to 82 percent in school 12.

It is also obvious that there is a range of performance within each school. What can be seen, but is less obvious visually, is that the higher-performing high schools have a smaller range of scores. The average range for schools 1 to 6 is 44 percent, whereas the average range for schools 7 to 12 is 26 percent. The minimum and maximum percent passing, and a visual indication of the ranges, are plotted in Figure 5.7 (page 158).

What still cannot be seen, however, is what the "normal" system capability is for this test. For that we have to resort to statistical process control procedures. This is not perfect statistical analysis. In fact, some of what is being suggested in order to "see" what data is saying would cause a statistician anguish. But that is the point. Most school leaders are not statisticians nor do they need to be. If one realizes that this data analysis is just a bit "squishy," it can still be used to point most nonstatisticians in the right direction. Of course, if exact figures are wanted, instead of squishy ones, learn statistics or hire someone who already knows it.

The concept behind a statistical process control chart (SPC Chart) is to determine what the upper and lower control limits of your process are. The variation between these two points is common variation that is attributable to your process. Any points above the upper control limit or below the lower control limit are the result of special cause variation and should be looked into immediately. Once special cause variation is eliminated, one can then work to improve internal aspects of the process, as in the case of schools, to raise both the upper and lower control limits. In the context of SPC, "control" only means that your process has an internal consistency, that it is predictable within limits, or that it is reliable. It does not mean that it meets your standard of expectations. Your process for teaching English, for example, may be well within control and highly stable but also far below the expectations, or requirements, you have for your school.

Upper and lower control limits can be computed using a variety of formulas, depending upon the qualities of the data being plotted. See Wheeler, Goal/QPC, or other sources to obtain the proper formula. Using the formula suggested in *The Memory Jogger*, an upper control limit (UPC) of 81.98 and a lower control limit of 54.02 are identified. These have been plotted and shown in Figure 5.8. Figure 5.9 shows these same upper and lower control limits added to the data presented in Figure 5.5.

As can be seen in Figure 5.9, there are 11 points above the upper control limit, 16 points below the lower control limit, and 45 points within the control zone. Everything between nearly 82 percent passing and 54 percent passing is normal or within control for this group of schools. If a school improved its regents passing percentage from 60percent to 80 percent, that would be considered within the range of normal variation.

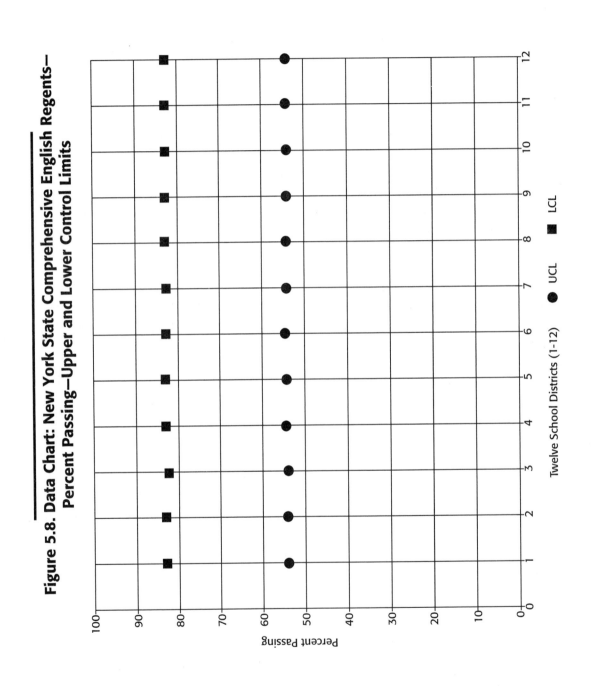

Figure 5.8. Data Chart: New York State Comprehensive English Regents—Percent Passing—Upper and Lower Control Limits

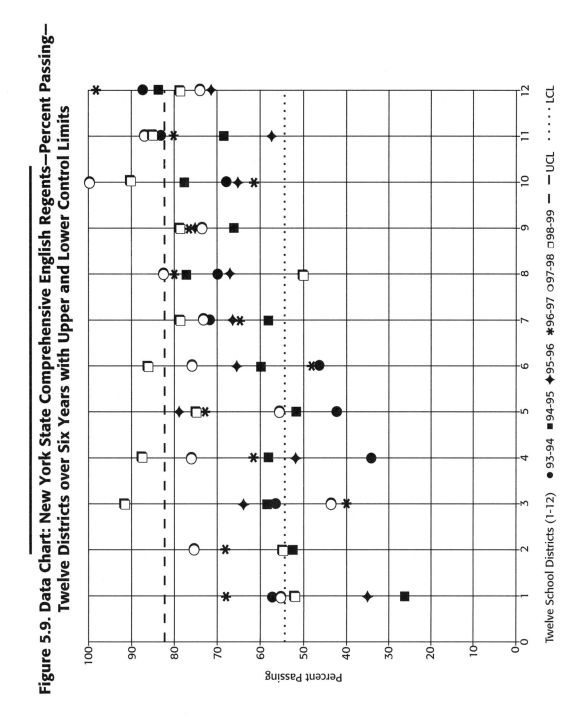

Figure 5.9. Data Chart: New York State Comprehensive English Regents—Percent Passing—Twelve Districts over Six Years with Upper and Lower Control Limits

Remember, these figures are a bit "squishy." The upper and lower control limits may be a point or two in either direction. What we are seeking is not machine-shop exactness as much as a global picture of what is happening.

In District 1, for example, three of its six data points are below the lower control limit, and two are very near the line. In fact, if one were to look at the passing record for this school district over the last six years, one would find that the aggregate percentage is actually below the lower control limit. On the other hand, district 12 has three of its data points above the upper control limit, and its aggregate six year percentage is actually very close to the upper control limit. There certainly appears to be special cause occurring in both districts—one of a negative nature and the other positive.

District 8 has generally performed above average for the region during the most recent year, 1998–1999, yet its results fell below the lower control limit. It would seem wise to investigate exactly what was happening. Is it a new teacher in need of immediate support? Is it just a totally different group of students? Was there something that happened in the district, such as a fire, that may have reduced time in class. What was the special cause that brought about this degree of variation?

In Districts 1 and 12, because the scores are more consistently low or high, it would appear that the special cause is something that the district is either doing or not doing in a consistent way. District 1 might very well want to benchmark with District 12 by asking "What do you think you are doing to achieve these results?"

In a more detailed search for differences among the 12 districts—information was compared on expenditures per pupil, teacher/student ratio, degree of poverty, size of district, and a variety of other factors that were identified as potential causes for what was happening. None of these seemed to be a factor. In fact, district 12 had the lowest cost per pupil. This same analysis was repeated for all other major state-assessed subject areas. It was interesting to note that the relative position of the 12 districts did not vary significantly from test to test. It was obvious that each district had its place in the pecking order. This was caused by specific factors that had to be investigated and either copied, as in the case of success, or dissolved where they caused failure.

Using elements from the diagnostic tree, the causes for high and low success should be found in one or more, or a combination, of: student demographics, curriculum, instruction, school processes, organizational culture, and, perhaps, external factors such as community demographics.

In a way, both benchmarking and statistical process control have been combined in this example. Working within a single district with a single high school program will make the charts and analysis simpler. Depending upon numbers, however, the variation may be so great as to make the result more than just squishy, and render it meaningless. The purpose of this example, however, is to illuminate the concept of variation and the need to separate what is common, or normal, variation, from that which is being caused by special factors that need to be attended to immediately. Once they are identified, the system can then be brought "into control" and can be worked upon to improve the process of instruction for all students.

In this example it is not logical to bring district 12 and the other successful districts "into control" but rather to use them to learn how to move the control limits for all districts toward higher percentages of success for all students.

An exercise such as this, combining benchmarking with the concept of statistical process control, also brings about greater understanding of one's own district and its needs for improvement.

Summary

This chapter presents a collection of independent thoughts that are essential fragments of the whole for using Root Cause Analysis in schools.

RCA can be used in any setting that requires answers to a problem, academic and nonacademic, from district-wide issues to those involving a single student. In each of these settings, however, leadership is essential.

Although RCA can be used as a tool in static settings, its purpose is to induce change by learning what we have to do differently in order to achieve our goals.

The timeline for any one RCA task will vary depending upon the complexity of the issue under study. RCA, however, can be adapted no matter the task. Gantt Charts are useful in monitoring the work of the team and in communicating it to all other stakeholders for purposes of verification and feedback.

RCA is most often conducted in the context of a school improvement committee or team that must have a clear charter of expectations, roles, and responsibilities.

Certain fundamental concepts and skills provide the necessary foundation for RCA. These are: systems thinking, understanding of the proper use of data, and understanding the importance of common and special cause variation and being able to differentiate between them.

6
Models and Stories

The continuous and reflective use of data undergirds the fundamental work of accountability. Schools with effective accountability systems examine their practices—with each other and with the broader community—routinely, explicitly, publicly, and collectively. The people who work inside such schools are committed to their own learning as well as that of their students. Guided by an ethic of continuous improvement to improve performance.

Using School Data for School Improvement, The
Annenberg Institute for School Reform

This chapter illustrates further the concept of root cause analysis in both school and nonschool contexts as a means of providing additional models for thinking about root cause. These models are:

- A *Multiple Measures Model* is an example of how a data search can be organized using Victoria Bernhardt's multiple measures of data. It also carries the process through to designing and implementing remedies (strategies) as well as evaluating their impact.

- The *Assessment Analysis Model* focuses on the process of assessment item analysis as an avenue to root cause.

- *Models of Nontraditional Data Sets* is a reminder that there are many data windows into the school system other than data generated by assessments and traditional indicators such as attendance, discipline, and dropout rates.

- *The National Transportation Safety Board—A Model* demonstrates how root cause analysis functions in the very real world of aviation disasters. A single tragedy reveals how multiple elements can often combine to cause a severe event.

The collection of *Root Cause Stories* is a random selection of tales based upon news articles of the type that can be found in nearly any daily paper, as well as some stories that have been told to, or that have been experienced by, the author over the years. Observations about each are reported for the purpose of illuminating further the use of root cause analysis in schools.

A Multiple Measures Model

Problem:

The state is moving gradually to require all diplomas to be academic. Most boys do not obtain academic diplomas.*

Student Learning Domain:

- Look at academic diploma data over the past 3 to 7 years.
- Look at standardized test scores by gender.
- What courses do boys not take?
- What academic requirements are they missing?
  - Is it by design (choice) or by result (failure)?

Demographic Domains:

- Collect data on other factors:
  - age
  - failure
  - economics
  - attendance
  - discipline
  - participation in extracurricular activities
- Are there differences by gender?

Perceptions Domain:

- Ask boys why they do not obtain academic diplomas.
- Ask girls why boys do not obtain academic diplomas.
- Ask parents why sons do not obtain academic diplomas.
- Ask staff why boys do not obtain academic diplomas.
- Examine the results—what is being said?

Process Domain:

- Curriculum, Content, Instructional Process
- Are retentions a factor? Failure?
- What about career plans?

Steps to Take

1. Generate "best hunches" as to what is causing this phenomenon

2. Test most plausible theories—the "Ah Ha's"

3. Search for root cause, asking the five whys

4. Design and implement remedy—research on best practice

5. Evaluate if remedy worked. If so, install within system.

*Data contained in Figure 3.6 (Hilltop Central School District)

Adapted from item developed by Ken Broadhurst—Capital BOCES, Albany, New York—using concepts from Victoria Bernhardt and the Juran Institute, 10/00.

An Assessment Analysis Model

Often, the search for root cause is initiated as the result of a single but crucial assessment. The model shown below parallels the Questioning Data process detailed in Chapter 3.

The Green Valley Central School is a relatively small district nestled within the mountains of upstate New York. Its fourth-grade students have taken the New York State English Language Arts (ELA 4) exam for the first time. The results are listed in Figure 6.1:

Figure 6.1. Results of ELA 4 Exam: Green Valley Central School

Level	Number of Students	Percent of Students
1	13	15.3
2	44	51.8
3	28	32.9
4	0	0
Total	85	100

In New York, student proficiency is rated from Level 1, the lowest, through Level 4, the highest. To successfully "pass" the assessment, students must score either a 3 or 4. Students at Level 2 are divided into "high twos" and "low twos" for purposes of determining their needs for additional support.

Data analysts warn repeatedly of small sample size and the high variability that can affect such small numbers. We are also warned about the need to make use of longitudinal data. Unfortunately, school districts are required to act regardless of their size and in spite of having only one data point for this newly implemented assessment. These are just two of the reasons why search for root cause within schools must often rely upon "squishy" data.

What can be "seen" immediately in this data set is that two-thirds of the students have not been successful on the assessment. It is also clear that no student scored at Level 4. These became immediate "red-flag" issues for this district.

What questions do we have about what we have seen in the data?:

- How do the students at Level 2 divide out into the high and low groups?

- Are there any differences in scores that are a consequence of student demographic issues?

- Are there any differences in scores that result from programmatic issues such as remediation, special education, classroom, etc.?

- What do teachers think about individual student scores in comparison to what they have observed, or assessed independently?

- What did the students think of the assessment? Were they "debriefed" immediately following its administration?

- Is instruction and the curriculum aligned with the assessment?

- What does a test analysis tell us? The analysis can be by state standard (listening, writing, reading), as well as analysis by item.

When the information from these various sources is compiled, shared, discussed and analyzed, no doubt certain patterns will emerge that will lead to areas of root cause. Our focus in this model, however, is the last question—"What does test analysis tell us?"

Too often, the immediate reaction is to conduct an item analysis and then to use the raw data from the analysis to identify possible inadequacies in either the curriculum or instruction. In New York, and other jurisdictions, this would be worse than wasted effort because the state assessments are designed using the concept of Item Response Theory (IRT). IRT is a tool of psychometricians that takes into account item difficulty. It can also take into account such factors as: (a) the ability of the question to discriminate, (b) guessing, and (c) the experience of the student in taking such tests. Using raw-item analysis can therefore be very misleading. A large number of students in a single school may fail to answer a specific question correctly, but that question may have been of high difficulty designed to differentiate between students deserving a 3 and those deserving a 4. How does one know which questions are easy and which are difficult? Unfortunately, many exams are secure and the details of scoring are obscured. In some regions, however, the systematic use of regional P-Scores has emerged as a means to judge how students within a district answered individual questions compared to all those within a region.

Simply put, *P-Scores* are a measure of the percentage of students who answered the question correctly expressed as a decimal. A P-Score of .86 indicates that 86 percent of the students in a region answered the question correctly. It was obviously an easy question. On the other hand, a P-Score of .34 indicates much greater difficulty because it means that only 34 percent of students within the region answered it correctly.

In order to properly conduct an item analysis on an assessment using IRT, one needs to compute the item P-Scores for the individual school and have on hand the item P-Scores for a sufficiently large region to guarantee reliability. A relatively small region in New York has a data warehouse of over 18,000 student scores for multiple years of testing that can then be compared to the responses of students in any one school district or building. By comparing local P-Scores with those of the region, one can obtain a fairly reliable picture of how the local students did in comparison to the much larger group on each question. By using the assessment item map provided by the state, one knows which skills are tested by each item. It is then a relatively simple task to identify specific content areas, skills, or standards as to which local students scored higher or lower than students in the region. This information can then be used to further explore local curriculum content, timing, and instructional methodologies.

Although P-Scores can be utilized in item analysis involving multiple-choice questions, they are not useful when examining student-constructed responses. There are several methods that can be used to examine constructed responses in sufficient depth to find causes for student failure.

Some school districts, and a few small regions in New York, have adapted the use of error coding. Each constructed response is typically scored on a scale of 1 to 3 or 1 to 4 using a statewide uniform rubric. All that is required is for the scorer to indicate the proper score for the response to each question. However, a score of 2, for example, provides minimal information. In districts that use error coding, the scorer also indicates the error or errors that the student committed that resulted in the less-than-perfect score. Each scorer works from a uniform listing of potential errors. To keep the error coding relatively simple, but still effective, a listing of four to six typical errors is uniformly applied to all constructed responses. By examining the pattern of errors, key information is supplied regarding areas of student weakness.

A second method is to allocate time for teachers to collectively review student constructed responses. Because many assessments are administered late in the spring, summer is a convenient time to allocate resources to bring staff in for such reviews. If assessments are administered earlier in the school year, time must be provided during the school year. Immediacy of response is important. Although the products of such collective review are not as quantifiable as those from error coding, they often provide broader insights into the issues underlying improper student responses. The process of collective review has its own benefit in terms of staff collaboration and better understanding of curriculum, state assessment, and student responses to specific prompts.

It must be cautioned that assessment analysis cannot substitute for a complete analysis of all possible root causes. It is but one avenue of discovery that often yields more questions than answers. If, for example, one discovers that students, no matter what their final score, are generally weak in one specific area of skills, the question "Why?" must be asked, and must be asked again for as many times as it takes to lead to fundamental cause. If one finds that one type of student is generally weak in a specific area of skills but that other students are not, the question "Why?" must be asked and continued until one finds the fundamental cause. Assessments, however, are an effective and proper window from which to observe student skills, and they cannot be ignored because they are frequently the means of state oversight and monitoring.

Models of Nontraditional Data Sets

Experience indicates that we all need to be reminded that there are numerous other types of data beyond assessment data that can be used to increase understanding of a school system and that can be employed to seek root cause.

In Chapter 3, Figure 3.1, teacher grading data was used to illustrate the Questioning Data Process. Teacher-given grades are most often used to measure student achievement and rarely to measure system success. Teacher-given grades are a powerful lens into the inner workings of the system.

Again in Chapter 3, Figure 3.6, another typically overlooked source of data—student permanent record cards—was used as an illustration. Like teacher-given grades, student permanent record cards collectively provide a wealth of information about the system but are most often used individually as a record of student progress over time. The permanent records of graduating seniors, for example, contain a fairly complete 13-year record of a single cohort of students.

In Chapter 5, a fairly traditional set of data—percent passing a state English exam—is made relatively unique by including data for six years from a cohort of 12 school districts, providing 72 data points. The longitudinal nature of this data set is not that typical and the benchmarking among 12 districts sets it further apart from the norm. Yet, much is gained by placing data in larger contexts of extended time and broader setting.

Perceptive data is not often collected, and is even more rarely used, within a constructive context such as a root cause analysis. Perceptive data can be sought from students, staff, parents, and community, depending upon the issue at hand. Any of the root cause processes will provide a proper context for deciding what perceptions to gather and how they will be used. Perceptions can be gathered by surveys, interviews, focus groups, and structured discussions.

School process data is likewise not often collected or used. One school district sought to examine the "process" of student participation in school-sponsored activities other than attending class. They conducted a review of student participation for three student cohorts from the time each cohort entered seventh grade until they graduated. The data set will be maintained and added to with each graduating class. Figure 6.2 displays summary data for the first three student cohorts.

Figure 6.2. Student Participation for Three Student Cohorts

	Enrollment			*Average GPA*			*Participation*		
Class of	*All*	*Male*	*Female*	*All*	*Male*	*Female*	*All*	*Male*	*Female*
1999	34	17	17	84.7	81.5	87.9	14.6	8.6	20.6
2000	37	14	23	86.8	82.5	89.4	18.8	11.4	23.3
2001	32	14	18	84.9	82.4	87.9	16.6	14.8	18.9

The first three boxes show enrollment for each of the cohorts and disaggregate enrollment by gender. Because this data is only for graduates, and not for all students in attendance in grades 7–12, it is affected by various factors such as students who have dropped out or did not graduate. Note that females represent 56 percent of the graduates and males represent 44 percent. A primary hypotheses, which would be simple to verify, is that the difference is caused by differences in the male and female dropout and graduation rates.

The center boxes show the average grade point average (GPA) for each cohort and the disaggregation by gender. Note that for each cohort, the female GPA is six to seven points higher than for males. In fact, 67 percent of all females were in the top half of their class, whereas 69 percent of males were in the bottom half.

The third set of boxes display data regarding student participation rates over the six years of secondary school (7–12). In the 1999 class cohort, females participated, on average, in 20.6 school extracurricular activities during grades 7I–12, whereas males on average participated in 8.6.

Correlations were run between the various elements with the results displayed in Figure 6.3.

Figure 6.3. Correlations of Cohort Data

GPA x Number of Activities	r = .672*
GPA x Gender	r = .492*
Gender x Number of Activities	r = .365*

*significant at the .01 level

Based upon the data in Figure 6.2 and 6.3, the following can be stated:

♦ Females participate in more extracurricular activities than males.

♦ Females obtain higher GPA's than males.

♦ There is a strong positive correlation between GPA and participation.

♦ There is a strong positive correlation between GPA and gender.

♦ There is a positive correlation between gender and participation.

♦ It appears that some males leave school without graduating.

Correlations do not necessarily point to causation but rather relationship. Perhaps some unidentified factor is causing girls to graduate more frequently, obtain higher grade point averages, and participate in far greater numbers than males. If so, what could it be?

This relatively simple tabulation of student participation rates, combined with information on their gender and grade point average opens a wide window into the culture of the school, and perhaps the community. It may simply confirm what many suspected, but, in such detail, it is difficult to ignore. If the school mandate is to enable all students to achieve high degrees of proficiency, what should be done when it appears that a significant category of student performs and participates at markedly reduced levels? What does this data say about student "engagement" with school? Where does this lack of male participation and lower achievement start? Can it be traced lower than seventh grade? These and many more questions can be asked if it is felt that it is sufficiently important to achieve the school's goals, as identified by its key indicators of success.

Data speaks, but it has to be converted to information, understanding, knowledge, and wisdom. The use of nontraditional data sets, and traditional data sets in nontraditional ways, enables the conversion.

The National Transportation Safety Board—A Model

Tragically, we have become all to familiar with the investigations of the National Transportation Safety Board (NTSB) as the result of recent airplane crashes. The NTSB is charged with determining "probable cause" for all U.S. civil aviation accidents, as well as selected highway accidents, fatal and/or passenger railway accidents, major marine accidents, pipeline accidents, and releases of hazardous material in all forms of transportation. Their procedures follow a detailed and classic process of root cause analysis and provide an excellent model for root cause analysis in other contexts, such as schools.

Not having access to specific NTSB manuals of procedures, one can infer the NTSB process by observing it at work through the eyes of the media. Figure 6.4 (page 174) presents a general approximation of the NTSB search for root cause for an air crash placed into the format of a diagnostic tree.

A diagnostic tree for use in schools was presented in Chapter 3, Figure 3.8 (page 67). The process here is the same, just the context is different. Each item in the tree must be proven as a contributing factor or sustained as noncontributing to the issue under investigation.

Figure 6.5 (page 175) presents information, again gleaned from the media, regarding a specific airplane crash—that of John F. Kennedy, Jr. off of Martha's Vineyard on July 16, 1999. The aircraft itself was found to be fully functioning and not a contributing or proximate cause for the crash. Seven intermediate factors are identified as either contributing or proximate to the cause of the crash. One deeper factor, the late arrival of a passenger, which caused the delay in takeoff, is also identified as a proximate cause. When all was said and done, the primary factors causing the crash involved pilot decisions and the lack of skills necessary to handle the conditions encountered near the end of the flight.

Figure 6.6 (page 176) presents the same information in the form of a flow chart with a summary listing of proximate, contributing and noncontributing factors. Flowcharts are handy tools for illustrating root causes.

Figure 6.4. NTSB Root Cause Simulation—Airplane Crash

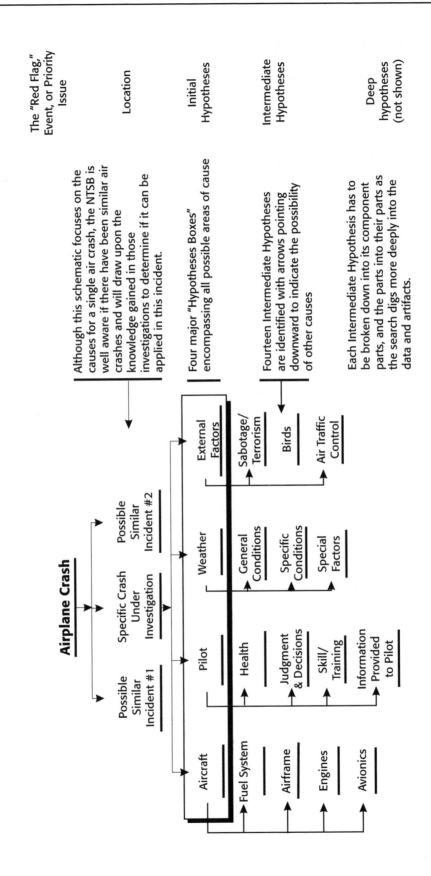

Figure 6.5. NTSB Root Cause Simulation—Airplane Crash of John F. Kennedy, Jr.

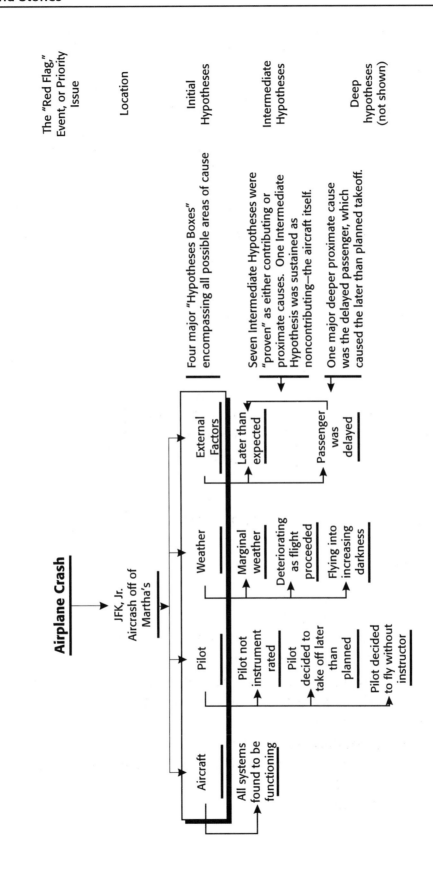

Figure 6.6. JFK, Jr.—A Brief Analysis of the Plane Crash

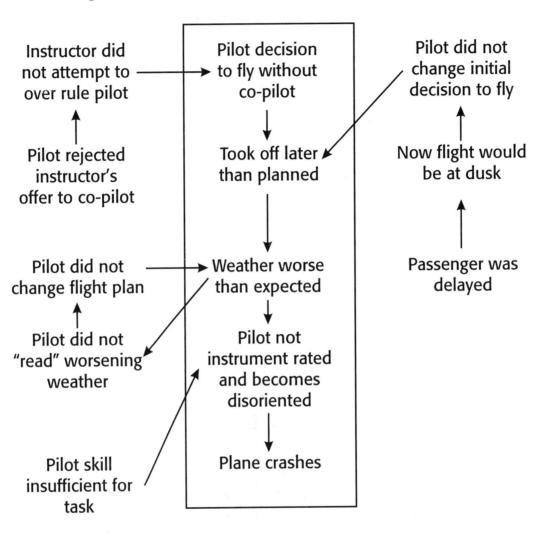

Proximate Causes:
 Delayed takeoff
 Hazy conditions over water at dusk
 Pilot not instrument rated
Contributing Factors: (root causes)
 Pilot judgement and decision making
 Pilot skill
Noncontributing Factors:
 Aircraft (engine, airframe, instrumentation, etc.)
 Weather Briefing
 Licensing

The NTSB report summary, ID NYC99MA178, available at http://www.ntsb.gov, presents the final determination of the accident's cause as: "the pilot's failure to maintain control of the airplane during a descent over water at night, which was a result of spatial disorientation. Factors in the accident were haze, and the dark night." Although this was the most immediate cause of the fatal crash, the chain of events leading up to the final loss of control over the aircraft started hours before while the pilot and passengers were still on the ground in New Jersey.

This tragic incident demonstrates the impact of how seemingly isolated and separate factors can become linked to produce an unwanted result. In this situation, for example, if any one of several factors had been absent, or other factors present, the crash would in all likelihood never have occurred.

The crash would most likely not have happened if any one of the following factors had been present:

- If the pilot had been skilled at instrument flying.

- If the flight instructor had been on board.

- If the pilot's decisions had been in keeping with skills and conditions.

The crash would not in all likelihood have happened if any one of the following factors had been absent:

- A late departure necessitating flying at night.

- Marginal weather that deteriorated during the flight.

- Pilot's decision to fly shortest route over 35 miles of water.

- Pilot's decision to continue flight as weather deteriorated.

It was the combination of these factors that placed the pilot in the situation of "spatial disorientation," which ultimately caused the tragedy. The accident would most likely not have occurred had any of the causes above been absent, or had any of the three potential preventative causes been present. It is not always necessary to remove all causative roots in order to prevent an incident, problem, or failure. It is just necessary to eliminate any one of the factors in the deadly combination. The fire triangle is a simple example. Fire requires the convergence of three items—(a) fuel, (b) oxygen, and (c) a source of ignition. Take away any one of the three, and fire cannot result. Oily rags cannot be kept out of a machine-shop environment; however, they can be contained in a covered steel pail where oxygen is limited and a source of ignition is remote.

In schools, isolated factors may often converge to create problems of heightened student failure. Through the process of root cause analysis, these isolated factors can be identified, and improvement efforts can then focus on dissolving the ones that appear easiest to deal with.

Root Cause Stories

The 10 stories that follow provide a diversity of contexts in which at least some evidence of problem solving is present. Much problem solving, however, is done without an understanding that it is, in fact, a search for cause. Causes for problems are often "found" as the result of "knee-jerk" reactions to data, and are based upon assumptions, attitudes, and/or beliefs rather than upon deeper analysis. Often "blame" or "fault" is sought rather than cause. Incomplete problem solving or root cause analysis frequently stops at immediate causal factors without digging more deeply to locate the fundamental causes.

There are at least three concepts that attempt to describe how causes interact, link, and connect to bring about the surface problem.

The first is the simple chain reaction concept, which can be easily described as "linear root cause." A simple example is the folk story of the missing horseshoe nail that resulted in the loss of the kingdom. The story provides a direct line of causation from lost nail, to lost horse, to lost rider, to lost battle, to lost kingdom. If any item in the chain is missing, the final reaction will not occur. This is sometimes also referred to as the "domino effect" or "cascading." Another interesting attribute is that every cause is also an effect. The lost battle is the cause for the lost kingdom but it is also the effect of the lost rider. Asking the "five whys" assumes the search for a linear chain of causation confined to a single line of discovery.

The second concept is that of "accumulating root causes." In this case, no single cause results in the full dimension of the ultimate problem; instead, a series of individual causes each contribute a certain share. A school with a dropout rate of 45 percent, for example, will most likely find that there is not a single cause for the total percentage of drop outs. Rather, individual causes, such as pregnancy, academic failure, family culture, school culture, economics, etc., may all be contributing causes to the ultimate problem of so many students leaving school before graduation. In order to solve this problem, each individual cause will have to be worked upon separately. Perhaps 15 percent of the issue is caused by girls who become pregnant and have few options to continue school once the baby is delivered and kept. If so, the 15 percent can be reduced by introducing different programs, but it will typically not help reduce the other 30 percent of drop outs that are caused by other things. When root causes "accumulate," each remains as a separate issue that is responsible for only a portion of the total result or symptom.

The third concept is that of "converging causes." In a convergent situation, we once again have separate elements, but, individually, they are typically benign, or at least not as bothersome. When combined, or when they converge at the same time and place, however, they can become explosive in bringing about an unwanted event. The concept of the fire triangle discussed earlier is an example of such converging causes. Paper, air, and matches are each relatively common and each is most often benign in its impact. But, strike a match and apply it to paper where there is plenty of air, and a fire is born. If the fire is in the hearth, the result can be quite pleasant. If, however, the fire is in a trash barrel, the result can be quite different. Likewise, although both driving and drinking entail certain separate risks, combine them within the same time and person, and there is an exponential increase in the potential for harm to occur. Phosphorous and water are relatively benign when separate, but when combined, they cause fire that is sufficiently hot to be of weapons' strength. To eliminate the problems caused by convergent causes, it is sufficient to keep them separated by as great a distance of time and space as necessary.

It is often possible to see all three concepts of cause operational within the context of a single problem issue. The operable concept, and the number of operable elements, will in part be determined by the complexity of the problem being examined, but will also be determined by the point of view upon which the study is based and the boundaries which are drawn around the event.

The discussion of these and other issues continues after the root cause stories are told.

Root Cause Story 1: Proctor High School (Utica, N.Y.) Lifted from Probation

In 1996, Utica's Proctor High School was named to New York State's list of "Schools Under Regents Review" (SURR) because of its high dropout rate. The annual rate for 1993–1994 was 14.7 percent and in 1994–1995 it was 14.6 percent. These rates were the third highest in the state. Being put on the list was a formal notice to the school that it could face state intervention or closure.

Red Flags:

High dropout rate coincident with the following:

♦ Failure in dropout record keeping.

♦ Students feared for their safety.

♦ State said Proctor lacked a caring environment.

♦ Discord between school and BOE, parents.

♦ Ninth graders were added with no advanced planning.

♦ Fights were common.

♦ Discipline was slack.

Root Cause Analysis:

♦ First step: learn who was dropping out and why.

Findings:

♦ Low attendance rates appeared as the first step out the door.

♦ Some foreign students—learning a new language and culture.

♦ High-school girls who became mothers.

♦ Those who wanted to earn money at a job rather than be in school.

Sample Strategies:

♦ Night School—143 students now take classes after hours—many are student mothers.

♦ A BOCES GED/vocational/job program.

♦ A "bridge program" with Mohawk Valley Community College.

♦ Ninth graders were returned to middle schools.

♦ A culture change at Proctor (caring).

  • Appearance

  • Student self-image

♦ A faculty mentoring program (70 faculty volunteers).

Results:

♦ Dropout rates dropped to 8.1 percent in 1995–1996, 7.7 percent in 1996–1997, 4.2 percent in 1997–1998, and 4.3 percent in 1998–1999.

♦ Proctor High School was removed from SURR List.

Source: Briggs, J. (2000, April). *Utica Observer-Dispatch.*

Root Cause Story 2: A First-Year Superintendent

In the first year of his tenure, a superintendent noticed that something was awry with the district's overall financial situation. Although his district's wealth was comparable to that of the neighboring district, the neighbor's facilities and equipment were notably newer, better kept, and superior. Not knowing why, he began to search the financial data of several comparable districts (benchmarking) to seek a reason (cause).

Red Flag:

- ♦ The appearance that the local school district's facilities and equipment were not up to par with a comparable neighboring school district.

Root Cause Analysis:

- ♦ Look for reasons in financial data.

- ♦ Benchmark local finances with several comparable school districts.

- ♦ Look for differences and clues in how money is spent and in the taxes and state aid received.

Findings:

- ♦ Other districts had far more indebtedness for capital projects.

- ♦ His local school district had no capital indebtedness.

- ♦ All updates, repairs, and major maintenance was being done with 100 percent local tax dollars on a cash basis in spite of the availability of nearly 70 percent aid on capital projects. In effect, for every dollar of local tax dollars spent, 70 cents was being lost.

- ♦ Local tax dollars were not being used efficiently to obtain state aid.

Strategies:

- ♦ The findings were shared with the Board of Education.

- ♦ A commitment was made to place all updates, repairs, and major maintenance into capital projects that would be bonded and become eligible for nearly 70 percent reimbursement.

Results:

- ♦ The first capital project was initiated, with a continuing series of projects culminating in the complete renovation of the high school and the building of a new middle school under the leadership of a future superintendent.

Source: *Experience*

Root Cause Story 3: The First-Year Principal

A the end of his first year, the high school principal was dismayed to see such a high percentage of student failure. He was determined to improve academic results and suggested to the faculty that the number of extracurricular activities that students participated in should be limited. It was noted that some students were engaged in four, five, and even six different activities, each of which obviously reduced the amount of time for study and homework. Although the faculty agreed, one educator suggested a deeper look at the data.

Red Flags:

- High percentage of student failure.

- Some students participating in many extracurricular activities.

Root Cause Analysis:

- Initially, the principal's interpretation of two sets of data—(a) failure rates and (b) participation rates.

- After the suggestion, a staff committee looked more deeply at failure rates and participation rates, linking them together.

Causal Factors:

- Although causal factors were not specifically found in this first analysis, it was determined that student participation was not linked to student failure. In fact, it seemed that those students with the higher participation rates were also those with the higher averages.

Next-Step Strategies:

- Cease jumping to conclusions based on opinion and cursory review of data.

- Initiate a root cause analysis for failure similar to that found in Chapter 3.

Source: Based upon self-revelations shared by the first-year principal.

Root Cause Story 4: The Wreck of the *Morning Dew*— A Tragedy That Should Have Been Avoided

On December 29th, 1998, the 34-foot sailboat, *Morning Dew*, steered a course out to sea, struck a jetty outside of Charleston, S.C. harbor, and sank. The skipper, his two teenage sons (aged 16 and 13) and a nephew (aged 14) perished.

Immediate Causal Factors:

- The skipper's decision to "go to sea."

- The boat was not equipped to "go to sea," and the trip at sea would be taken at night.

- The weather was stormy with heavy rain and winds of 15 to 20 m.p.h. Seas were four feet.

- A second adult had left the crew in response to a family emergency the day before.

- The boat had an inexperienced, ill-equipped, and inadequate crew.

- The skipper had been "on watch" for 17 hours. Perhaps he was severely fatigued and hypothermic.

- The skipper did not follow his original plan to use the Inter-Coastal Waterway.

- No float plan was filed.

Reconstructed Time Schedule and Actions:

- 2:17 A.M.—US COAST GUARD (USCG) RECEIVED MESSAGE ON EMERGENCY VHF CHANNEL.

  - Watchstander was at the coffee machine and misheard message.

  - Watchstander did not play back the message, thinking it was just a test.

- 2:21 A.M.—USCG received a second message, but it was just static.

  - Watchstander tried to respond but received no answer. Neither call was logged.

- 6:20 A.M.—Incoming boat hears cries for help coming from the water. Crew searches—finds nothing.

- 6:28 A.M.—USCG notified, but does not send a boat because pilot boat is already in area.

  - Pilot boat searches area—does not see or hear anything. It remains in area until daylight.

- 6:38 A.M.—USCG notified that nothing was found. USCG takes no further action.

- 11:00 A.M.—COUPLE FINDS FIRST BODY WASHED ASHORE. SECOND BODY IS FOUND A SHORT TIME LATER.

- 11:15 A.M.—POLICE NOTIFY USCG THAT BODIES HAVE WASHED ASHORE.

  - USCG duty officer is concerned that the 6:28 call and the 11:15 call are related.

- 11:44 A.M.—PILOT BOAT FINDS MAST STICKING OUT OF THE WATER IN GENERAL AREA.

- 11:46 A.M.—USCG HELICOPTER IS DISPATCHED.

- 11:48 A.M.—USCG 41-foot utility boat is dispatched

- 12:46 P.M.—USCG helicopter spots a third body.

- The skipper's body would not be found for 24 more days.

♦ 4:15 P.M.—Watchstander mentions the possibility that the 2:17 radio call might be related.

Contributing Causal Factors to the Fatalities (NTSB):

♦ Watchstander was at the coffee machine instead of at his station—could not hear the Mayday.

♦ Watchstander did not replay the tape.

♦ USCG had no formal procedures to guide the Watchstander.

♦ USCG did not train the Watchstander to use "all available means" to follow up on calls.

♦ USCG staffing policy should have required two people on watch—not one.

♦ USCG required Watchstander to stand a 12-hour watch—alone.

♦ NTSB found that a large number of personal calls are made by Watchstander.

♦ USCG has no program to evaluate districts or Watchstanding

♦ USCG tape recorder was difficult to use to replay messages—hence messages were not replayed.

  - Tape recorder could not be used to search for a specific message.

  - Not replaying the tape was a crucial factor in negating a rescue.

♦ USCG Direction Finder was inadequate and, therefore, was shut down.

Source: Seaworthy. (2000, April). *BoatUS*, 18(2).

Root Cause Story 5: Follow-Up to the Wreck of the *Morning Dew*—A Tragedy That Should Have Been Avoided

On December 29th, 1998, the 34-foot sailboat, *Morning Dew*, steered a course out to sea, struck a jetty outside of Charleston, S.C. harbor, and sank. The skipper, his two teenage sons (aged 16 and 13), and a nephew (aged 14) perished. From the May 2001 BoatUS Magazine:

A Federal Judge has found fault with the US Coast Guard's failure to launch an adequate rescue of the stricken sailboat *Morning Dew* near

Charleston Harbor and has awarded the skipper's widow and sister-in-law damages of $19 million.

In his 64 page opinion, US District Judge David Norton wrote, 'This tragedy was avoidable.... It was not an angry sea or cruel weather that impeded the Coast Guard's ability to rescue the *Morning Dew's* passengers. It was human error, the impetuous termination of a search and rescue mission approximately 30 minutes before sunrise.'

An investigation after the accident revealed that Daniel Cornett radioed a mayday call at 2:17 A.M. A Coast Guard petty officer tried to return the call but got no reply; he later said he did not hear a "mayday" in the scratchy transmission. However at 6 A.M., crew on a commercial vessel entering the harbor reported to the Coast Guard that they heard cries for help from the water. A pilot boat in contact with the Coast Guard conducted a search but found nothing. The Coast Guard did not send out any units until the bodies of two of the boys were found at 11 A.M."

Norton ruled that if a search had been conducted, the boys might have been saved. No damages were awarded for the death of the father, Michael Cornett, because it was assumed he was thrown overboard when the vessel hit the jetty and could not have been rescued.

Source: (2001, May). *BoatUS*, 6.

Root Cause Story 6:
What Has Happened to the Recruits?

The U.S. Armed Services are having a retention crises of record proportions. Over the years, 30 percent of recruits have been leaving before their first term is up. But now, a record 36.9 percent of 1994 recruits have left before conclusion of their term in 1998. Basic training costs $40,000 per recruit plus another $1000 for recruitment costs. Nearly $250 million has been lost.

Red Flag:

♦ A retention crisis of record proportions.

Root Cause Analysis:

♦ None reported. The inference, however, is that databases of causes for recruits leaving were used.

Immediate Causal Factors:

♦ Loneliness

- Mother's cooking
- Don't like the hours
- Mental and physical stress
- Unaccustomed to orderliness
- Discipline and expectations
- Fraudulent enlistment (25 percent)
- Physically out of shape
- Injuries (foot—caused by boots)
- Drugs

Sample Strategies:

- Three-day "think it over program" at U.S. Army Fort Jackson.
- Three-week conditioning program prior to basic training at U.S. Army Fort Jackson.
- Changed philosophy at Fort Jackson—"We won't give up on them."
- Boot camp lengthened to nine weeks instead of eight—giving laggards extra time.
- Trainees wear boots one day, sneakers the next—Lakeland Air Force Base
- New sports medicine clinic at Marine's Parris Island base—takes sting out of injury.
- Air Force has decreed that overseas assignments max out at 90 days every 15 months.
- Marines—pre-boot camp physical "resorts."
- Fingerprint checks before enlistment.
- Air Force—Retention is a function of leadership: advancement depends on retention rates.

Sample Results:

- Salvaging 2,500 recruits out of 36,000 passing through Fort Jackson
- Injuries halved at Lakeland Air Force Base

Source: Omicinski, J. (2000, April). *Utica Observer-Dispatch.* Washington, DC: Gannett New Services.

Root Cause Story 7: Welcome Freshmen!

The proportion of high-school graduates attending college has increased from 49 percent to 63 percent (1980–2000) resulting in a more diverse population, more students working to pay for college, and greater impact of expanding freedom found at college.

Red Flag:

At public colleges, nearly 60 percent of all freshmen fail to obtain degrees within five years of entering. Half of those leave the first year. Dropout rates are higher at many community colleges.

Root Cause Analysis:

Thirty years of experimentation and data used to identify factors leading to dropout rates.

Immediate Causal Factors (extrapolated from identified strategies):

- ◆ Lack of faculty mentoring and skill in supporting marginal students.
- ◆ Lack of intimacy/caring on large campuses—students get lost.
- ◆ Students do not come prepared with organizational and study skills.
- ◆ Students find it hard to "connect" with others with similar interests.

Strategies:

- ◆ Training faculty to mentor and support new students.
- ◆ Creating first-year seminars, orientation, courses, and intimate learning communities.
- ◆ Teaching students organizational and study skills.
- ◆ Arranging dorms so that freshmen live among students with similar academic interests.

Sample Results:

- ◆ 71 percent of more than 4,000 accredited campuses offer first-year seminars.
  - • 85 percent of freshmen take them.
  - • Survival rate of participants is 3 to 10 percent better than those who do not participate.
- ◆ Indiana University: The percent of freshmen returning for sophomore year increased from 80 percent to 85 percent from 1994 to 2000. Freshmen retention of African-American and Latino students has jumped from 64 percent to 82 percent.

- Appalachian State: Freshmen enrolled in seminars return at a rate of 90 percent, compared to 84 percent for those who do not enroll. More than 50 percent of class enrolls in seminars.

- Seattle Central Community College: Students enrolled in learning communities return at a rate of 90 percent, compared to college's overall retention rate of 70 percent.

Source: Omicinski, J. (2000, April). *Utica Observer-Dispatch.* Washington, DC: Gannett New Services.

Root Cause Story 8: Firestone Recalls ATX and ATX II and Wilderness Tires—August 9, 2000

Firestone tires had been under investigation by the National Highway Safety Administration since May 2nd after a flurry of complaints and reports of four deaths in accidents allegedly caused when the treads peeled off the tires and caused the vehicles to skid or roll over.

Red Flag:

- 46 deaths blamed on 3 Firestone tire models.

Root Cause Analysis:

- Process not reported upon.

Immediate Causal Factors:

- Although temperature and speed are not considered to be the only factors, the greater number of tire peelings have occurred in warm-weather states at highway speeds.

Suggested Contributing Causal Factors:

- Steel belted radial tires constructed in the U.S. since the 1970's have a faulty design—chaffing of steel belts against the rubber tread loosens tread.

- The adhesive bonding the tread to the tire is not good enough.
  - Climate control in the factory—high humidity causes poor bonding.
  - At certain times, the adhesive turns to powder.

- Quality control in the Firestone plants.
  - Most faulty tires come from one plant.
  - The same plant has had labor problems.

- Workers are now working with a contract extension while negotiating.

Suggested Strategies:

♦ Place nylon safety layers (cap) between steel belts and the tread.

- Cost = $1 per tire.

♦ Improve adhesive, and control humidity during bonding process.

♦ Ensure high levels of quality control.

Source: (2000, August 9). *USA Today*.

Root Cause Story 9:
Ammonia Leak Case Settled

A railroad tanker leak occurred in Fort Edward, New York, in August of 2000 requiring the evacuation of more than 1,000 residents for three days. The 30,000 gallon tanker was transporting ammonia from Canada to a paper mill in Glens Falls, New York, when the leak developed, spreading a toxic cloud of gas over much of the Village of Fort Edward. It took nearly three days to cap the leak.

Red Flag:

♦ Ammonia leaking from a parked railroad car in Fort Edward, New York.

Root Cause Analysis:

♦ Trinity Railcar Repair, Inc., found at fault, as the result of improper repair.

Immediate Causal Factors:

♦ Worker incorrectly repaired a valve on top of the tanker, July 17, 2000.

- Used an improper gasket (which either gave way or dissolved)
- Replaced bolts in a reverse position.

The Search for Other Contributing Causal Factors:

♦ Why was the worker assigned to this type of repair not properly trained to do it?

♦ Why wasn't the unskilled worker more properly supervised?

♦ Why didn't quality control catch the error?

Imposed Remedies:

♦ Fines and restitution of $924,000.

♦ The U.S. Department of Transportation is also requiring Trinity to initiate "various remedial actions designed to maximize tank car safety and avoid future accidents."

Source: (2002, November 22). The Glens Falls Post Star.

Root Cause Story 10: Jury Asked to Determine Blame

A teacher is fatally shot in a Florida school, and a 13-year old student is found guilty as an adult and sentenced to 28 years in prison. Because of an additional suit against the gun distributor, the jury was asked to determine the amount of blame that the gun distributor had for the incident. It was hoped that this would become a landmark case against the weapons industry.

Red Flags:

The shooting incident and death of the teacher.
The "Saturday night special" in the hands of a 13-year-old.

Root Cause Analysis:

The jury process went beyond the intent of the plaintiffs and assigned "blame" in the following manner:

The gun distributor	5 percent of blame	$1.2 million
The school board	45 percent of blame	$10.8 million
The gun owner	50 percent of blame	$12.0 million

Possible Neglected Causal Factors:

♦ What about the student—does he have no blame?

♦ What about the parents—again no blame?

♦ What about violent video games, TV, and movies?

♦ What about the National Rifle Association?

♦ What about places of worship?

♦ What about the neighborhood?

♦ What about the bullet and gunpowder makers?

♦ What about society in general?

Possible Strategies of Prevention:

♦ Use gun detectors and inspectors at school doorways?

Source: Based upon Albom, M. Commentary. *The Detroit Free Press*. [Reprinted 2000, November 19, in *Post Star*, Glen Falls, NY].

Root Cause Stories: A Review

The story of Proctor High School, Root Cause Story 1, tells the result of what appears to have been a relatively informal search for cause, namely: "First step: learn who was dropping out and why." Yet, it contains all of the elements of a more structured organizational process. Once certain trends were found, strategies were specifically selected to reduce the impact of each of those trends. The dropout problem is an example of accumulating causes bringing about an unwanted result.

The first-year superintendent, in Root Cause Story 2, was in the process of learning the financial "ropes" of the district. A more experienced superintendent may have been able to identify the cause by simply scanning the books. Nevertheless, the new superintendent knew what he did not know and used benchmarking as a tool to discover new knowledge about his district. In its simplest form, the root cause configuration in this tale is mostly linear. The Board of Education and previous superintendents had seen fit to fund all updates, repairs, and major maintenance with local tax dollars rather than to establish building projects that would be funded largely through state aid. The sole use of local dollars, and the loss of state aid over time, resulted in an accumulating deficit in the quality of local facilities. As the facilities aged, they required ever-increasing amounts of local funds to maintain. These funds, in turn, had to be taken from limited local tax revenues, which meant that other aspects of the educational program received fewer dollars.

Such benchmarking processes can be used to find similarities and differences between one's own system and others for the purpose of illuminating nearly any school process, from instructional results to maintenance of the boilers.

The story of the first-year principal, in Root Cause Story 3, illustrates more about how schools often respond to issues than it does about root cause analysis. It illustrates what can happen if analysis of cause does not take place and if raw data is not converted to information, knowledge, understanding, and wisdom.

The Wreck of the *Morning Dew* is a tragic and complex story (Root Cause Story 4). It involves at least two root cause issues: (a) the cause for the wreck and (b) the cause for the failure to respond by the United States Coast Guard. Let's take them in sequence. The immediate causal factors are many. Some may think of them as an accumulating stack of elements that each, separately, contributed to the wreck. Looking more closely, however, one can see that each immediate causal factor would probably not have caused the wreck on its own—it was the combination, or convergence, of the many isolated negative factors that almost guaranteed failure. Although each of the many immediate causes may indeed have a linear path of causes leading to it, the overall pattern is one of multiple, separate causes that converged to cause the tragedy.

In focusing on the failure to respond, it is easy to blame the Watchstander as the most immediate cause in this situation. He, or she, can be thought of as lounging around the station, getting coffee, make a "large number" of personal calls and generally being rather bored and inattentive to the frantic call for help. He did not hear the message clearly when it was received and did not bother to replay the tape. Perhaps the Watchstander must share some burden of causation, but when the context of his work environment is examined, we find more fundamental causes. He has had no formal training; no formal procedures were established for Watchstanders to follow; he was standing a 12-hour watch alone; there was no process evaluation or review of his work or of his function; and the tape recorder was difficult to use. One could argue that this is another example of accumulated causes resulting in a negative event. However, a good argument can be made that if any one of the missing elements had been present the search would have been timely and successful. If, for example, there were two people on the watch, chances are the initial message would have been followed up on, or perhaps even heard the first time through. If the tape recorder had been easier to operate, chances are that it would have been used more frequently. If the training, procedures, and supervision had been of a higher standard, the Watchstander might have better understood the importance of his role. Asking another "why?" could very well lead to even deeper latent causes within the culture of the USCG. As seen in the follow-up Root Cause Story 5, the court found the United States Coast Guard guilty of failing to launch an adequate rescue.

Like the Watchstander, teachers often are the focus for blame for student failure to learn. If one looks more closely, however, student failure is more a reflection of the failure of the whole system. Who attracts and recruits the teachers? Who recommends and employs the teachers? Who supervises and evaluates the teachers? Who recommends teachers for tenure? Who provides teachers with continuous and ongoing training and support? Without these elements being present and vital, it is difficult to place fundamental blame for student failure in the lap of the teacher.

The captain of the *Morning Dew* no doubt embarked upon his journey with high hopes, sincerity, and good will. The convergence of his decisions and other elements, however, brought about the tragic result. The same can be true with leadership in any school that has high hopes of bringing about school reform. The staff may be inexperienced, the infrastructure of the system may not be up to the task called for, plans may not be in place or followed, or decisions may be made in the heat of conflict or by default. School improvement is not any easy task, and it should be approached with all of the skill, knowledge, and tools that can be assembled. Root cause analysis is one of those tools.

The loss of nearly 40 percent of armed services recruits is told in Root Cause Story 6. Again, accumulated data is used to seek cause for recruits leaving the service prior to the end of their term of enlistment. Multiple immediate causal factors are found and strategies are targeted at the causes. Because each cause can operate independently, this is an example of accumulating causes bringing about such a magnified effect. One can think of a pie chart in describing the separate contributions of each causal factor. Each contributes to the whole but remains independent in its ability to influence the result.

Welcome Freshmen! (Root Cause Story 7) tells a tale very similar to that of the loss of recruits. Again, data from over 30 years, as well as results of previous efforts, are used to identify specific strategies aimed at dissolving cause. Again, the causes are cumulative rather than converging.

The story of Proctor High School, the loss of military recruits, and the loss of college freshmen all have a common theme: the general attrition of a specific population over time. The root cause analysis processes in all three stories are similar: find out why people are leaving and address each of the accumulated issues with some sort of strategy to reduce its contribution. A similar problem can be found in certain instances in the high attrition of beginning teachers, administrators, or even members of boards of education.

The Firestone tire tragedy (Root Cause Story 8) is yet another example of cumulative causation, although in this case, the number of causes are limited. One might make an argument that the cause is also linear as demonstrated with the following questions and answers, based on factual allegations:

- ♦ Why do Firestone tires cause accidents?
  - Because their tread peels off, causing vehicles to roll over.
- ♦ Why do their treads peel off?
  - Because of high temperature and speed.
- ♦ Why do high temperature and speed cause the treads to peel off?
  - Because the steel belts chaff against the rubber tread and loosen the tread, and
  - Because the adhesive bonding in the tire is not good enough, and
  - Because climate control in the factory causes poor bonding, and
  - Because quality control in a single factory is substandard.

By the time one gets to the third "Why?," however, one can see that there are multiple, separate, causes—any one of which can cause the tread to break away from the tire. This is yet another example of accumulating causes that require separate strategies targeted at each.

The story of the Firestone tires offers an example of how changing the "Why?" question can change the whole nature of the search for cause. In addition to asking the second "Why?" regarding the peeling of treads, another "Why" could have been: "Why do the vehicles roll over?" Is it necessary that a vehicle roll over when its tire tread peels, or is there something also wrong with the vehicle. Those that recall the debate between Firestone and Ford will remember this exact line of reasoning. Are the accidents caused by the combination of an improper tire placed on vehicles that are less stable? By improving the tire, the margin of safety has perhaps been widened, but the complete solution cannot be obtained until the vehicle itself becomes more stable.

In school, we can identify the misalignment of curriculum with the standards as a fundamental cause for student failure on an assessment that is aligned. We can seek fundamental, perhaps even latent causes, for why the curriculum was not aligned in the first place. But there is a second line of questioning that must be asked: are instructional techniques also aligned with the standards? If not, the lack of instructional alignment becomes as critical to failure as does the lack of an aligned curriculum.

At one level, Root Cause Story 9 reports upon a linear series of causation. Using the "five whys" we can travel down this pathway.

- Why did the railroad tanker leak?

  - A faulty valve.

- Why was the valve faulty?

  - It had an improper gasket and was bolted incorrectly.

- Why were the gasket improper and the bolts incorrect?

  - A repair worker incorrectly replaced the gasket and bolts.

- Why did the repair worker perform the task improperly?

  - Lack of proper training and supervision.

- Why was this error not caught?

  - Quality control missed the improper gasket and bolts.

One can travel down the root cause path in a linear fashion until the fourth and fifth "whys," when the causes start to become multiple. However, if one were to continue with the sixth and additional "whys," one might find a corporate culture or climate that set the stage for all of the above. A demand for high production rates, for example, could cause lack of training, lack of supervisory staff, and missed quality control checks. (Similarly, what are the possible "latent" causes for problems of student achievement?)

Our final story, "Jury Asked to Determine Blame" (Root Cause Story 10), illustrates just how complex finding cause within a social context can be. Although the jury assigned blame to three possible causal factors, the writer of this commentary questions why many others were not included. Can we ever know the deep roots for an act such as this with any degree of clarity? At the very basic level, the student pulled the trigger and will serve a sentence of 28 years for this act. If the gun had not been easily stolen and/or used, the shooting might never have taken place. If the school had had greater security, would the gun have ever entered the building? It is doubtful that the jury used any formal process to arrive at blame, but instead relied upon their ability to agree on certain beliefs, attitudes, and perceptions about such a crime. It will be interesting to follow the case on appeal. Are there convergent factors in this story? Yes. Are there accumulating factors? Yes. Is there a linear cause and effect? Yes. It all depends on the scope and point of view of the inquiry.

Although risking the thought that root cause analysis is an impossibly complex waste of time for schools, these stories are shared with the hope that they can clarify the use of root cause analysis, and the lack of, or misuse of, causal identification. It is obvious, however, that the search for cause is necessary to identify proper strategies for solution and that there are systematic tools that can be used. Causes come in patterns—sometimes in strings, other times in aggregates, and, in other instances, separate, benign, causes lay around waiting to converge. Causes are sometimes close to the surface and are relatively easy to find, whereas others are buried deep within the culture of the system. As schools gain insight, experience, and increasing skill in asking "why?," in seeking cause, and in converting data to wisdom, their efforts to improve will have increasingly greater positive impact on student learning. Seeking and eradicating causes for poor performance should be the way schools go about all of their business.

Summary

In this chapter, we look at several models and stories that serve to illustrate root cause analysis in real-world contexts. There is no one right way to conduct the discovery process for root cause. There are, however, incorrect ways to respond to problems. "Knee-jerk" responses to initial data, assigning blame, and not digging deeply enough are all impediments to seeking cause and to solving the problem.

State assessment results are increasingly the focus of many school improvement efforts. Though they are an important consideration, and a source for much insight into the school system, analysis of assessment results must be made with full knowledge regarding the specific assessment under study and with the realization that it is only one window for viewing the system.

Nontraditional data sets, data sets that are not usually used to better understand a system, are valuable portals for gaining greater understanding of how the system functions and what possible causes might be. Data about perceptions and school processes are often neglected. Teacher-given grades and permanent record card data are just two of many often overlooked sources for data.

The National Transportation Safety Board (NTSB) process of finding "probable cause" has become an all too familiar model for discovery of root causes for airplane crashes. A detailed discussion of the John F. Kennedy, Jr. crash in July of 1999 was used as the context for examining how the NTSB's model parallels the concept of the Diagnostic Tree discussed in Chapter 3 and how the same information can be converted to a flow chart.

Root causes can occur in a chain of linear events or elements; separate causes can accumulate, each contributing its own share to the final result; or separate elements can converge to cause a result that no one of the elements can cause on its own. Ten root cause stories were told to illustrate the various real-world contexts for seeking cause and how these three formations of cause can be identified and sought.

7

Resources

To lead an organization beyond the status quo, leaders must confront the realities about people and organizations that mitigate against systemic change. Doing so injects tension into the system, which can be uncomfortable, but only leaders who can capitalize on the organizational energy created by this tension and use it constructively to lead systemic change will truly be effective.

Jerry Patterson, *Coming Clean about Organizational Change*

Why These Resources Are Essential for Understanding Root Cause Analysis

In many texts, the three items that follow—the Glossary, the Bibliography, and the Web Sites—are frequently relegated to the appendices or some such section beyond the main body of the text. They are included here as the final chapter as an indication that they are an essential part of learning about root cause. They should not be bypassed.

As indicated in Chapter 2, educators do not have a common vocabulary. Words may have different meaning in different contexts. Teams seeking to solve problems often assume the words being used have the same meaning for everyone on the team. This is seldom the case. The Glossary defines terms used in this guide and should be used as a tool for gaining common agreement on the meaning of words used by the RCA team.

Mark Twain is quoted as saying, "The man who does not read good books has no advantage over the man who cannot read them." Others have indicated that in order to function as a leader, one must first become a reader. The Bibliography lists over 50 texts that I have found meaningful in both my pursuit of root cause and in linking root cause analysis to the process of continuous school improvement. As explained later, the texts represent a diverse collection covering at least six general themes. Knowledge of the content in each of these themes is most helpful for those who wish to successfully lead, facilitate or implement root cause analysis.

Although Web sites often disappear, and links to them then lead to nowhere, it is impossible to think of resources today without including the vast array of sites available on the Internet. Just over 50 sites have been identified. A link to the sites of the 50 state education departments is also provided. The nature of most of these links is such that they should remain open for some time to come. Like the texts, the links cover a wide spectrum of organizations and content. Each site is related in its own way to the ongoing process of continuous school improvement. The additional linkages provided within each of these sites creates what amounts to an ever-expanding network of supporting sites containing a vast amount of information.

These resources should be used to develop a broad foundation for the implementation and use of root cause analysis for solving real problems in the context of real schools.

Glossary

In education, the same term often has many different meanings. Misunderstanding is caused by the lack of common definition of terms. It is important that a uniform definition of key terms be developed as part of any school improvement process. This glossary is an attempt to provide specific "contextual" meaning for many key terms. As the school improvement process unfolds in a specific location, new terms will emerge. It is essential that those leading the process ensure that each new term is defined and that the common definition be spread throughout the organization and used uniformly.

Action Plan:	The product of a root cause analysis process that identifies the strategies to be implemented to dissolve the root cause and who is going to do what on what schedule and with what resources to implement each strategy. Also called an "implementation plan." Can be plotted using a modified Gantt Chart.
Assessment Analysis:	A pathway for seeking root cause for student failure—examination of the assessment including: item analysis, content mapping, and alignment with standards, curriculum, and instruction.
Back Room Data:	Data as it is used to seek root cause is often exploratory, messy, complex and filled with unnecessary detail—as opposed to presentation data, which should be clear, concise, and focused on major findings.
Benchmarking:	A process by which a school district compares the measures of its key indicators with those of several similar districts to determine how well it is doing in comparison to others. If other districts are achieving better results, a benchmarking visit or consultation should be undertaken to learn how the better results have been achieved.

Brainstorming:	A tool used in root cause analysis to identify what team members think are potential areas of underlying causes. More generally, a structured process for generating ideas from all members of a group.
CDEP	Comprehensive District Educational Planning—a process piloted and adopted by over 150 school districts in New York State.
Cohort	Used to describe a single assemblage of students, most often a whole grade level, e.g., an entering ninth-grade "cohort."
Common Cause Variation:	Variation within a process that is a normal part of the process. All processes vary. Common cause variation is normal variation.
Contributory Causal Factor:	An alternative to the term "root cause" suggested by Medical Risk Management Associates that results from the complexity of many situations where no single "cause" can be found but rather a number of separate factors contribute in combination to the problem or gap. Also called "Root Contributor." See Fundamental Root Cause.
Control:	A process is said to be in control when special cause variation is eliminated and only common cause variation is present. In this state, the output of the process can be predicted within certain specified limits, known as upper and lower control limits.
Control Chart:	Used in statistical process control (SPC) to show the output of a process over time, and, when computed, the upper and lower control limits of the process. Sometimes called a run chart.
Control Limits:	A derivative of standard deviation that shows the predictable upper and lower limits of a process's output. All variation within these control limits is considered normal. Variation either above or below the control limits is considered to be special cause variation.
Creative Root Cause Analysis:	A group process of root cause analysis developed by Dr. Jack Oxenrider of the Dow Leadership Development Center at Hillsdale College consisting of a series of structured steps, including the development of a probing question followed by team problem solving and team communication cycle.
Culture:	School culture is a complex composite of history, values, assumptions, norms, and attitudes that manifest themselves in school climate and artifacts such as policies, procedures, methods, styles of communication and processes. Cultural elements are often "latent" causes.

Data Warehousing:	A system of storing large amounts of data electronically over time for the purpose of rapid retrieval and querying. A very useful tool for examining large amounts of data in order to find cause.
Data Set:	Used to describe any collection of data that describes a relatively narrow set of outcomes, such as attendance rates.
Data Swamp:	That large morass of school-generated data that is often compiled in different locations and formats and that contains information both significant and insignificant. Without the use of a guide, such as a Key Indicators of Student Success, getting lost in the data swamp is relatively easy.
Desired Ideal Condition:	The condition we should all strive for—the perfect result—such as 100 percent attendance or successful completion of a course, grade, or diploma requirements. Often used as the target for school improvement efforts.
Diagnostic Tree:	A root cause analysis tool that provides a guided structure for digging deeply to find cause. Main branches include: student demographics, curriculum, instruction, school processes, and school culture.
Disaggregation:	The process of taking basic Level One data and breaking it apart into smaller components based upon identified key factors. Student test data, for example, may be broken down or disaggregated by age, gender, ethnicity, sending school, zip code, language spoken, etc.
Ends:	Ends are the purpose of school, not the strategies, materials, methods or other means of achieving them. Essential ends are most clearly stated as Key Indicators of Student Success.
Error Coding:	A process whereby student-constructed responses on assessments are not only scored for correctness, but, when less-than-perfect, are coded according to a uniform set of errors. Error coding provides detailed information about "why" students responded incorrectly.
Fishbone:	A graphic tool that shows the relationship among the many causes of a problem. Also called a cause and effect diagram or an Ishikawa diagram.
Five Whys, The:	A simple process used to seek root cause by asking "Why" five times in succession.
Flow Chart:	A chart that graphically shows the flow of a process. Used as a tool to explain, verify, and communicate exactly how a process functions.

Force Field Analysis:	A process whereby the driving and restraining forces acting on a system are identified and placed on a graphic for visual consideration. The theory indicates that the system will move in the direction wanted by removal, or decreasing, the restraining forces rather than by building the driving forces only, which will create increased pressure. A tool for discussing and presenting root cause issues.
Fundamental Root Cause:	The deepest cause or causes that can be found—most often located at the systems level.
Gap:	The difference between desired student performance outcomes and actual student achievement.
Gantt Chart:	A horizontal bar chart developed by Henry Gantt in 1917 to assist in production control. In addition to identifying the party responsible for each element, it provides a useful means for monitoring implementation action plans and communicating what is to be accomplished when and by whom.
Goal Statement:	A statement that identifies a student key indicator (performance goal), the target, and a timeline for achieving it.
Implementation Plan:	The product of a root cause analysis process that identifies the strategies to be implemented to dissolve the root cause and who is going to do what on what schedule and with what resources to implement each strategy. Also called an action plan. Can be charted using a Gantt Chart.
Immediate Cause:	The most immediate, obvious or superficial cause of a problem. Usually located close to the event. A "proximate cause."
Key Indicator:	A selected measure of a school's success that has been formally identified, publicly verified, and that is monitored as part of an ongoing school improvement planning process. Most typically, they are student-focused, measurable outcomes that the school has the ability, desire, or need to influence and for which it is willing, or required, to be held accountable.
Latent Causes:	A concept, developed by C. Robert Nelms, that there are often underlying, hidden causes that cause people to do what they do. Nelms identifies latent causes as attitudes, assumptions, and beliefs.
Levels of Root Cause:	Root causes can be found at ever deeper layers of the school. Levels include: the incident, program, whole system, and external causes.
Level One Data:	The initial aggregated data set, prior to disaggregation or further analysis. Used to identify "red-flag" issues.

Level Two Data:	A deeper data set, usually a disaggregation of an initial set of aggregated data. As Level Two Data is further disaggregated and analyzed, it becomes Level Three Data, etc.
Longitudinal Stream:	The concept that data in schools must be viewed over many years in order to understand the system and to seek root cause.
Lower Control Limit:	A computed number that indicates the predictable lower limit of a process's output. Any output below this limit is considered to be special cause variation and is an indication that the process is out of control.
Item Response Theory (IRT):	A psychometric tool that can take item difficulty, ability to discriminate, guessing, and the test-taking experience of the student into account when scoring an assessment.
Means:	The "things we do" in order to achieve our goals (ends). In schools, this will include items such as methods and materials of instruction, curriculum, staff development, scheduling, budgeting, assessment, planning, communication, and special programs and processes.
Modalities of Root Cause:	Although root cause analysis is most frequently used in a negative reactive mode (looking back to find out why something went wrong), it can also be used in at least three other modalities. In the positive reactive mode, one looks back to find out what went right. In the positive proactive mode, one looks forward to learn what has to be in place for a new process to be successful. In the negative proactive mode, one looks forward to learn what has to be dissolved for a new process to be successful.
Multiple Measures of Data:	Dr. Victoria Bernhardt has provided this very useful model of the multiple types of data that are used in Root Cause Analysis. They are: student achievement data, student demographic data, school system and process data, and stakeholder perception data. Often, a single data set, such as student grades, can be used both as a measure of student achievement and also of the school system and its processes.
Need:	Needs are gaps in student learning (achievement) between where students should be and where they actually are.
Noncontributory Factors:	Factors that, upon investigation, seem not to have contributed to the problem or gap, but that are noted in order to document that they have been explored.

P-Scores:	Simply the percentage of students in a sample that answered a specific multiple-choice question correctly. Where P = .75, 75 percent of the students answered the item correctly. P-Scores are used to determine item difficulty and the degree to which local students responded correctly as compared to a much larger regional cohort.
Paretoing:	A tool used to "weight," through voting, the various factors identified as possible root causes. The pareto concept is that 80 percent of the result comes from the most important 20 percent of the factors (e.g., 80 percent of class cuts come from 20 percent of the student body).
Patch:	A "solution" that deals only with the symptom or proximate cause rather than with the root cause. Patching results in increased cost and complexity and does not dissolve the fundamental problem.
Performance Goal:	A target for a specific level of student performance to be achieved with a specified time frame. Usually tied to a key indicator of student performance and a specified measure, such as an assessment.
Presentation Data:	Data presented to stakeholders should be clear, concise, and focused on major finding,s as opposed to working back room data, which is often messy, complex, and filled with unnecessary details.
Problem:	A situation where performance does not meet expectation.
Process:	All work is process. A process consists of input, value-added action, and output. Once one can identify all three components, the process can be defined. The term "process" is used to define a mini-system nested within a larger system (e.g., instructional processes within the school system).
Proximate Cause:	The most immediate, obvious, or superficial cause of a problem. Usually located close to the event. An immediate cause.
Questioning Data:	A process used to seek root cause by "seeing" what data has to tell and then identifying "questions" about what is seen as a basis for further investigation.
Red-Flag Issue:	Something in a data set that causes the reader to assess that something significant is happening (or not happening) and that needs to be investigated further. Usually, an obvious discrepancy between expectation and result.

Root Contributor:	An alternative to the term "root cause" suggested by Medical Risk Management Associates that results from the complexity of many situations where no single "cause" can be found but rather a number of separate factors contribute in combination to the problem or gap. Also called Contributory Causal Factor.
Root Cause:	The deepest underlying cause or causes of positive or negative symptoms within any process, which, if dissolved, would result in elimination, or substantial reduction, of the symptom.
Scattergram:	A tool used to display the correlation or interaction of two variables on a chart. Also called a scatter diagram.
Special Cause Variation:	Variation within a process that is not normal (unique) and is typically caused by some type of special event or circumstance.
Stable Process:	A process that exhibits only common cause variation.
Standard:	An agreed-upon and established statement of expectations for students—focused on issues of learning, attitude, and behavior. Standards drive key indicators.
Statistical Process Control (SPC):	A system for monitoring process outcomes that separates common system variation in outcome from special cause variation by enabling the computation of upper and lower control limits for a process.
Symptom:	The most immediate visible sign of a problem (need).
System:	A simple system consists of an input and a valued-added activity, resulting in a defined and expected output. Complex systems consist of many such processes, linked together, to form a complex outcome. Systems nest within systems (class, course, department, school, district).
Systems Thinking:	A way of viewing the whole rather than just a part. Understanding the interrelationship of all the parts to each other and that the whole is not the sum of the parts but rather the product of how the parts are linked.
Target	A student performance goal that a school sets and that should indicate a score (rate) and a timeline for reaching that score (rate).
Team:	A group that is dynamic and working together toward a well-defined goal. Implies greater linkages and engagement than a committee.

Timeline: A tool used to graphically display a sequence of events.

Triangulation: A process of gathering multiple data sets to focus in on understanding an issue rather than relying upon a single form of evidence. Multiple forms of data provide a more distinct and valid picture of reality.

Underlying Cause: Those causes that contribute to the proximate cause.

Unstable Process: A process that is "out of control" as a consequence of special cause variation.

Upper Control
Limit: A computed number that indicates the predictable upper limit of a process's output. Any output above this limit is considered to be special cause variation and is indication that the process is out of control.

Variation: Differences in process outcome over time. Variation may be either common cause (normal) or special cause (unique). In working to improve systems, it is important to understand and identify what kind of variation is present.

Verification: The process by which a team product is publicly disseminated and reviewed for the purpose of using the input generated to modify the product before it becomes finalized.

Bibliography

There are literally hundreds of potential texts that can be used to expand one's understanding of root cause, systems, and the use of data to improve schools. The sampling below are those that have helped to form my knowledge and skills in this and related areas. I am indeed indebted to these authors for enabling me to support, verify, and expand my own concepts as I travel the same pathway to improved learning for all students.

Although the texts listed focus on a variety of issues, each in its own way contributes to the process of school improvement. The texts can be grouped according to the following general themes:

♦ Data gathering, processing, and analysis.

♦ How to conduct surveys, gather opinions, and use qualitative data.

♦ Root Cause Analysis.

♦ Statistical tools and processes.

♦ Foundational concepts such as Quality and Systems Thinking.

♦ Processes for school improvement.

Anderson, G. L., Herr, K., & Nihlen, A. (1994). *Studying your own school: An educator's guide to qualitative practitioner research.* Thousand Oaks, CA: Corwin Press.

Annenberg Institute. (1998). *Using data for school improvement: Report on the Second Practitioner's Conference for Annenberg Challenge Sites.* Houston, TX: Author.

Bernhardt, V. (1998). *Data analysis for comprehensive schoolwide improvement.* Larchmont, NY: Eye On Education.

Bernhardt, V. (1999). *The school portfolio: A comprehensive framework for school improvement.* Larchmont, NY: Eye On Education.

Bernhardt, V. (2000). *Designing and using databases for school improvement.* Larchmont, NY: Eye On Education.

Bernhardt, V. (2000) *The school portfolio toolkit: A planning, implementation, and evaluation guide for continuous school improvement.* Larchmont, NY: Eye On Education.

Bernhardt, V., Von Blankensee, L., Lauck, M., Rebello, F., Bowilla, G., & Tribbey, M. (2000). *The example school portfolio.* Larchmont, NY: Eye On Education.

Blazey, M. L., Davison, K. S., & Evans, J. P. (1999). *Insights to performance excellence in education 1999: An inside look at the 1999 Baldrige Award criteria for education.* Milwaukee, WI: Quality Press.

Bonstingle, J. J. (1992). *Schools of quality: An introduction to total quality management in education.* Alexandria, VA: Association for Supervision and Curriculum Development.

Bracey, G. W. (1997). *Understanding education statistics: it's easier (and more important) than you think.* Arlington. VA: Educational Research Service.

Brassard, M. (1996). The Memory Jogger Plus+. Methuen, MA: Goal/QPC.

Cicchinelli, L. F., & Barley, Z. (1999). *Evaluating for success: Comprehensive school reform—an evaluation guide for districts and schools.* Aurora, CO: McRel.

Cox, J. (1996). *Your opinion, please!—How to build the best questionnaires in the field of education.* Thousand Oaks, CA: Corwin Press.

Creighton, T. B. (2001). *Schools and data: The educator's guide for using data to improve decision making.* Thousand Oaks, CA: Corwin Press.

Delavigne, K. T., & Robertson, J. D. (1994). *Deming's profound changes: When will the sleeping giant awaken?* Englewood Cliffs, NJ: Prentice Hall.

Deming, W. E. (1982). *Out of the crisis.* Cambridge, MA: MIT Center for Advanced Engineering Study.

Doyl, D. P., & Pimentel, S. (1999). *Raising the standard: An eight-step action guide for schools and communities.* Thousand Oaks, CA: Corwin Press.

Fields, J. C. (1993). *Total quality for schools: A suggestion for American education.* Milwaukee, WI: ASQC Quality Press.

Fitzpatrick, K. A. (1997). *School improvement: Focusing on student performance.* Schaumburg, IL: The National Study of School Evaluation.

Fitzpatrick, K. A. (1998). *Indicators of school quality: Vol. 1. Schoolwide indicators of quality.* Schaumburg, IL: The National Study of School Evaluation.

Gano, D. L. (1999). *Apollo root cause analysis: Effective solutions to everyday problems every time.* Yakima, WA: Apollonian.

Glasser, W. (1995). *The control theory manager*. New York: Harper Business.

Goal/QPC. (1996). *The Memory Jogger Plus for education*. Methuen, MA: Author.

Holcomb, E. L. (1999). *Getting excited about data: How to combine people, passion, and proof*. Thousand Oaks, CA: Corwin Press.

Holcomb, E. L. (2001). *Asking the right questions: Techniques for collaboration and school change*. Thousand Oaks, CA: Corwin Press.

Jenlink, P. (1995). *System change: Touchstones for the future school*. Palatine. IL: Skylight Training.

Johnson, R. S. (2002). *Using data to close the achievement gap*. Thousand Oaks, CA: Corwin Press.

Joint Commission on Accreditation of Healthcare Organizations. (2000). *Root cause analysis in health care: Tools and techniques*. Oakbrook Terrace, IL: Author.

Kanji, G. K. (1999). *100 statistical tests*. Thousand Oaks, CA: Sage.

Kaufman, R., & Herman, J. (1991). *Strategic planning in education: Rethinking, restructuring, revitalizing*. Lancaster, PA: Technomic.

Latino, R. J. , & Latino K. C. (2002). *Root cause analysis: Improving performance for bottom-line results*. New York: CRC Press.

Leithwood, K., Aitken, R., & Jantzi, D. (2001). *Making schools smarter: A system for monitoring school and district progress*. Thousand Oaks, CA: Corwin Press.

Leonard, J. F. (1996). *The new philosophy for k–12 education: A Deming framework for transforming america's schools*. Milwaukee, WI: ASQ Quality Press.

Levesque, K., Bradby, D., Rossi, K., Teitelbaum, P. (1998). *At your fingertips: Using everyday data to improve schools*. MPR Associates and the National Center for Research in Vocational Education and the American Association of School Administrators.

Love, N. (2000). Using data—getting results: Collaborative inquiry for school-based mathematics and science reform. Cambridge, MA: TERC.

McCary, M., Peel, J., & McColskey, W. (1997). *Using accountability as a lever for changing the culture of schools: Examining district strategies*. Greensboro, NC: SERVE.

Murphy, C. U., & Lick, D. W. (2001). *Whole-faculty study groups: Creating student-based professional development*. Thousand Oaks, CA: Corwin Press.

Newton, R. R., & Rudestam, K. E. (1999). *Your statistical consultant: Answers to your data analysis questions*. Thousand Oaks, CA: Sage.

Patterson, J. (1997). *Coming clean about organizational change: Leadership in the real world*. Arlington, VA: AASA.

PQ Systems. (1998). *Total quality tools for education (K–12)*. Miamisburg, OH: Author.

Preskill, H., & Torres, R. T. (1999). *Evaluative inquiry for learning in organizations*. Thousand Oaks, CA: Sage.

Schlecty, P. C. (1990). *Schools for the 21st century: Leadership imperatives for educational reform*. San Francisco: Jossey-Bass.

Schlecty, P. C. (1997). *Inventing better schools: An action plan for educational reform*. San Francisco: Jossey-Bass.

Schmoker, M. (1999). *Results: The key to continuous improvement*. Alexandria, VA: The Association for Supervision and Curriculum Development.

Senge, P. M. (1990). *The fifth discipline: The art and practice of the learning organization*. New York: Doubelday.

Senge, P. M., Kleiner, A., Roberts, C., Smith, B. J., & Ross, R. B. (1994). *The fifth discipline fieldbook: Strategies and tools for building a learning organization*. New York: Doubelday.

Short, P. M., Short, J., & Brinson, Jr., K. (1998). *Information collection: The key to data-based decision making*. Larchmont, NY: Eye On Education.

Slavin, R. E., & Fashola, O. S. (1998). *Show me the evidence! Proven and promising programs for American schools*. Thousand Oaks, CA: Corwin Press.

The University of the State of New York. (2001). *Data analysis and improving student performance*. Albany, NY: The New York State Education Department.

Thomas, S. J. (1999). *Designing surveys that work: A step-by-step guide*. Thousand Oaks, CA: Corwin Press.

Tucker, S. (1996). *Benchmarking: A guide for educators*. Thousand Oaks, CA: Corwin Press.

Wahlstrom, D. (1999). *Using data to improve student achievement: A handbook for collecting, organizing, analyzing and using data*. Suffolk, VA: Successline.

Wheeler, D. J. (1993). *Understanding variation: The key to managing chaos*. Knoxville, TN: SPC Press.

York-Barr, J., Sommers, W. A., Ghere, G. S., & Montie, J. (2001). *Reflective practice to improve schools: An action guide for educators*. Thousand Oaks, CA: Corwin Press.

Annotated Listing of Web Sites

Today, a world of information is literally just a few clicks away on the Internet. The Web is an essential tool for school leaders, and the sites listed below are just a small portion of all those that are related to the subject of school improvement. Collectively, however, they provide a wealth of information and a multitude of links to related sites. Each of these sites should be considered as a portal to the never ending, and intertwining, path of discovery required for continuous school improvement.

The listing consists of four parts.

1. Sites of general interest to those leading school reform efforts

2. A listing of the Regional Educational Labs, each of which has special areas of emphasis and which provide a wealth of current information and research.

3. A single Web site that provides links to all of the state education departments as well as those of the territories.

4. A collection of sites related to the issue of data collection warehousing and analysis. Efficient root cause analysis ultimately depends on the ability to store, mine, analyze and present student and school data with relative ease.

Sites of Interest

http://www.annenberginstitute.org	The Annenberg Institute for School Reform, based at Brown University, is working on urban school reform based on the following strands: rethinking accountability, engaging the public, and building the capacity of school professionals to reform schools.
http://www.ascd.org	The Association for Supervision and Curriculum Development is a membership organization focusing on issues of teaching and learning for the success of all students. ASCD publishes a free, daily, e-news briefing on educational issues that can be subscribed through this site.
http://edreform.com	The Center for Education Reform (CER) is an independent advocacy organization that provides support to all who seek fundamental reforms in schools. A free weekly "Newswire" is available via e-mail. This is a fine example of the call for reform.
http://www.clsr.org	The Center for Leadership in School Reform (CLSR)—The Schlecty Group— focuses on the quality of work provided students by their schools. Dr. Phillip C. Schlechty created CLSR as a means of supporting leaders of school reform efforts.
http://www.makingstandardswork.com	The Center for Performance Assessment is a private educational organization that helps individuals, school districts, and corporations achieve their educational objectives through assessment, accountability, and standards.
http://www.cse.ucla.edu	The Center for Research on Evaluation, Standards, and Student Testing (CRESST) conducts research on important topics related to K–12 testing. Funded by the U.S. Department of Education and the Office of Educational Research and Improvement.

http://www.emsc.nysed.gov/rscs/laplans/Innovative/CDEP/cdephomepage.htm	The New York State Education Department's homepage for Comprehensive District Education Planning (CDEP).
http://accelerateu.org/cdep/index.cfm?Group_ID=0&SessionID=138	The CDEP Technical Assistance Center's Web site.
http://corwinpress.com	Corwin Press—source of books in the Bibliography, above.
http://nccsso.org	The Council of Chief State School Officers works on behalf of the state education agencies governing K–12 schooling in the United States.
http://www.creativerootcauseanalysis.com	Dr. Jack Oxenrider's Creative Root Cause Analysis (CRCA) site providing information on the process and training for conducting RCA.
http://www.ctb.com	CTB McGraw Hill Glossary of Assessment
http://ers.org	Educational Research Services (ERS)—a nonprofit foundation serving the research and information needs of educators and the public. A rich resource for educational information.
http://www.ecs.org	The Education Commission of the States' (ECS) mission is to help states do together what they could not do near so well alone. This is accomplished through the sharing of news and information, policy research and analysis, conferences, technical assistance, publications, and support for networking and partnerships. The site maintains highly developed links to a wide variety of educational resources on the Web.
http://nces.ed.gov/edfin	Education Finance Statistics—a division of the National Center for Educational Statistics (NCES).
http://eff.csuchico.edu	Education for the Future Initiative (EFF) is led by Dr. Victoria Bernhardt, and is the "portal" to obtaining her many books and services. EFF's mission is "to support and build the capacity of schools to provide an education that will prepare students to be anything they want to be in the future."

http://www.edtrust.org	The Education Trust—the site contains their data guide and State and National Data Book on schools.
http://www.eyeoneducation.com	Eye On Education publishers—source of books in Bibliography, above.
http://childstats.gov	Forum on Child and Family Statistics—contains information on "Key National Indicators of Well-Being" for youth and includes 25 indicators in the areas of: economic security, health, behavior and social conditions, and education.
http://www.hbem.com/library/glossary.htm	The Harcourt Glossary of Measurement Terms
http://www.nces.ed.gov	The National Center for Educational Statistics (NCES) is the primary federal organization for the collection of national and worldwide education-related data. The site contains a data tools section that facilitates access and manipulation of data.
http://www.ed.gov/NLE	The National Library of Education is the "world's largest federally funded library devoted solely to education" and "is the federal government's main resource for education information."
http://www.nsdc.org/index.html	The National Staff Development Council is a membership organization "committed to ensuring success for all students through staff development and school improvement." This Web site has special sections for parents, as well as a school improvement library with extensive links.
http://www.orionhealthcare.com	Location for "Root Cause Analyst:" an automated root cause analysis product for the health care industry.
http://deming.ces.clemson.edu/onlineq.html	Location for an "Online Quality Resources Guide" with many links to information about W. Edwards Deming and the Quality movement.
http://www.plan2020.com	The author's Web site and contact point.
http://www.rootcauselive.com	A Web site devoted specifically to the tools and use of Root Cause Analysis. Practitioners from many fields contribute.

http://www.yahoogroups.com/group/rootcauseconference/join	A Root Cause discussion group located at Yahoo. A varied group of participants all interested in Root Cause Analysis.
http://www.schoolmatch.com	Schoolmatch is a school research and database service firm that specializes in rating schools (K–12) for parents, corporations, and schools. Launched in 1995 this Web site is designed to provide access to school information.
http://spcpress.com	Dr. Donald Wheeler's Web site on statistical process control.
http://www.wglasser.com	The William Glasser Institute. "The mission of the William Glasser Institute is to teach all people Choice Theory and to use it as the basis for training in Reality Therapy, Quality School, education and Lead-Management."
http://www.census.gov	The U.S. Census Bureau—the key portal to Census 2000 data.
http://www.ed.gov	The U.S. Department of Education—No Child Left Behind—provides access to the USDOE and NCLB Web sites that are filled with interesting and essential information.

The Regional Educational Laboratory Network

| http://www.relnetwork.org | The Regional Educational Laboratory Network Homepage

■ A network of 10 regional laboratories supported by the U.S. Department of Education that was implemented by Congress over 30 years ago as part of the Elementary and Secondary Education Act. Each laboratory is distinctive in its focus but also maintains common elements. Together they provide a rich resource for those seeking improvement of learning for all students. |

State Departments of Education

| http://www.ccsso.orgseamenu.html | All state sites are listed at this CCSSO link page. |

Data Warehousing: Examples and Resources

http://www.escholar.com	E-Scholar provides software to handle school data entry from diverse sources and to query data for decision making.
http://www.escholar.com/eScholar-NYS-PR.htm	A press release from E-Scholar announcing its selection as the standard data warehouse and data analysis solution for K–12 education throughout New York State.
http://www.cnyric.org/sitemap.htm	The Central New York Regional Information Center homepage. An example of the services offered by the 12 regional information centers of New York State including Cognos PowerPlay Web cubes.
http://www.cognos.com	The Cognos Web site. Many schools in New York State are using Cognos supported data mining and querying processes to inform their decision making.
http://www.spss.nl/datamine	The SPSS Web site containing information on data mining in schools.
http://dataview.wnyric.org	The Western New York Regional Information Center Data Warehouse & Data Analysis page.
http://www.ease-e.com	The homepage for Tetra Data's Ease-E school data warehousing, mining, analysis, importing, and training programs and services. An example of the state-of-the-art in school data management.

Also available from Eye On Education

**Using Data to Improve Student Learning
in Elementary Schools (with CD-ROM)**
Victoria Bernhardt

**The School Portfolio Toolkit:
A Planning, Implementation, and Evaluation Guide
for Continuous School Improvement (with CD-ROM)**
Victoria Bernhardt

Data Analysis for Comprehensive Schoolwide Improvement
Victoria Bernhardt

Designing and Using Databases for School Improvement
Victoria Bernhardt

**The School Portfolio: A Comprehensive Framework
for School Improvement, 2nd Edition**
Victoria Bernhardt

**The Example School Portfolio:
A Companion to the School Portfolio**
Victoria Bernhardt, et al.

Achievement Now! How to Assure No Child Is Left Behind
Dr. Donald J. Fielder

**Navigating Comprehensive School Change:
A Guide for the Perplexed**
Thomas Chenoweth and Robert Everhart

**Measurement and Evaluation:
Strategies for School Improvement**
James McNamara, David Erlandson, and Maryanne McNamara

**Better Instruction Through Assessment:
What Your Students Are Trying to Tell You**
Leslie Walker Wilson

The Call to Teacher Leadership
Sally J. Zepeda

Implementation: Making Things Happen
Anita Pankake

School Community Relations
Douglas J. Fiore